THE AQUARIUS AGE

Gali Lucy

The information contained in this book is in no shape or
form a diagnosis, prescription or treatment of any health
disorder whatsoever. This information simply presents a
suggestion or an opinion of the author and should not
replace consultation with a competent healthcare
professional. In the case of any medical, mental or
psychological problem one must consult proper health care.
The author and the publisher are in no way liable for any
misuse of the material.

Table of Contents

Divine Message 1

All of you shall care for one another and be as one and I shall gather you from the four corners of the world. I shall uplift your souls from the gutters, to lead you from despair and doom, with the ancient knowledge to ' Tikkun Olam', repairing the world.

Righteousness and purity shall cleanse your thirsty souls, to prepare you for the future, teach you the secrets and unite your souls. In the distant future, I shall wash your faces in a turbulent ocean, earthquakes, and signs.

This book is for the generations, contains my words. There is no anger, fury or punishment - all of me is love.

I prayed to God:
"Let me have everything so that I may enjoy life".

& God replied:
"I gave you life - so that you may enjoy everything".

A folk saying

This message was received through channeling...

Divine Message 2

Dearly beloved,
who are asking for assistance and guidance in your lives,
so you may understand where you should turn to next.

Go to the wise and silent person,
who does not ask for alms or provides you with talismans,
who does not walk wearing fine clothes or spends his time
in temples and luxurious buildings.

You will reach that person by word of mouth.
Be wise, go to the modest, quiet, and humble ones.

The words of wisdom of heaven are spoken quietly
with humor and a smile, not with shouting, threats
and intimidation.

Not by might nor by power, but by spirit,
I am the LORD.

This message was received through channeling...

Introduction

This book was written using male pronouns, yet it is intended to apply to both genders. I would like to thank all those who purchased, received, or borrowed this book. Nothing is coincidental!

This book was transferred to me during channeling and typed directly into the computer. It was written to satisfy the public's curiosity with insights and knowledge which my soul has collected through its thousands of incarnations. All that is required of you the reader is curiosity, flexible thinking with a healthy sense of humor, and a willingness to accept new ideas.

Do not believe this book but find your own truth, because there will never be one truth in order to provide you with a free will to choose.

The purpose of this book:

Based on my second book 'The Future', I decided to go into detail in this book regarding 'The Aquarius Age', which is one out of the 12 Zodiac ages listed in the book. **We are now** separating from 'the Age of the Pisces' and gradually **entering 'The Aquarius Age', which will begin in the year 2106 and last until the year 4212.**

It is important for each person to receive explanations about the changes taking place around him and what is expected for the future of humanity on Earth.

Before we begin, here arc a few basic insights:

- **There never was and never will be a single truth,** because it denies the right to choose. If there was only one truth - you would have been prevented from thinking otherwise; therefore, accept the contents of this book as additional opinions which can enrich the knowledge you already possess.

It is important that you create your own personal opinion and way of thinking, open your mind, and never blindly follow other people's ideas, but research.

- **You are all spirits made of souls,** temporary guests inside human forms across the universe.

- **Nothing was nor ever will be yours, other than your free will.** Even your soul is not yours, but was lent to you, in order for you to complete your destiny.

- **Life is like a game of monopoly:**
Each player (a living human being) begins at the starting point (birth) with a backpack (his soul's journey) and a roadmap which contains the player's chosen main lines of his destiny, combined with the soul's secondary lines, which are created by the player during his life.

During this game, the player undergoes changes, buys /
sells, builds / separates, ascends / descends, finishes the
game's round (dies) and returns to the starting point (the
soul 'returns home' to God). Then it starts all over again
(the soul is reborn in a new body or remains as a spirit)
with a new roadmap (the lines of destiny) in a new
location somewhere on Earth or in some other location in
the infinite universe. In your original source you are not a
soul, but a ball of light. A soul is inside a living human
body. A spirit is when a soul is outside the body.

• **Your aim is to endlessly recreate.**
You are all originally a spirit. You chose to be embodied
in **material** living bodies for a short time, in order to
<u>testify to the nature</u> of your **soul**:

  ▪ Who you are as a spirit.

  ▪ The nature of *The Creation*.

• **God can never be ONE!**
The universe always allows a free choice between at least
two options, that's why **God is not one but multiple
universes** which constantly duplicate themselves.

• **No material will make a soul happy for long, only
emotions will.**

• **You cannot die.**
You are originally made of spirit which cannot be
extinguished. You're all eternal souls.

- *"All is foreseen, but freedom of choice is given".*

A question may come to mind:
"If all is foreseen - then where is the person's choice?"

And the answer is:
"The Creation (God) will never interfere in the human's choice. A divine pattern exists with the main destiny lines of each person, while there is free will to select each move."

For example, imagine driving a vehicle on an existing road which has multiple paths (= all is foreseen) yet **the right to choose** how and where to drive between those paths through interchanges and shortcuts **is given to you,** the driver (= freedom of choice is given).
You can lengthen or shorten your road, but eventually, you will reach the same target foretold.

- **All will happen - only time changes.**

- **All the diseases originate from the soul.**
A spirit cannot be cured using only material; therefore, medicines (drugs) can't cure in the long term, but can only silence the problem, which stems from the person's soul. In order to truly heal, you must combine the work of a medical professional with a diagnosis of a medium and treatment from a healer.

• **In every Galaxy, life can exist only on one planet!**
Therefore, from the nine planets in the solar system, life can exist only on planet Earth.

The astrological sign of the Zodiac contains the order of the 12 Ages, which affects the nine planets surrounding the sun in the Milky Way Galaxy, including planet Earth - The only planet on which life can exist.

• **All religions involve material and violate free will.**
Spirituality cannot be religious because the spirit is the opposite of material.

A religious man: deals with material: houses of worship, books, talismans, ceremonies, religious artifacts, and clothing.

A spiritual man: does not deal with religion or material but communicates with *The Creation* / God without any additional accessories, but with modesty and inner quiet.

• **You do not need any mediators.**
All of you are associated with *The Creation* (God) once you have been created. You are all an infinite spirit with a soul that was lent to you for your journey in a tangible body.

• **The humankind on Earth was created by The *Creators* =** the Extraterrestrials, while planet Earth serves as an experimental lab. **You are a soul** (spirit) which embodied in a human body (material) **to testify the** nature of you - as a spirit, in order to testify to the nature of *The Creation* (God). (Divine Creation /2016).

• God is not in the religions - but in the spirit of faith.

• God did not create religions or time - humanity did.

• God can never be ONE – otherwise, you won't have options to choose from.

• There are no religions in the universe, but free will.

• Religions get a tremendous impetus during the Age of the Pisces which began with the birth of Jesus in the year 0 and continues until the year 2106. The Aquarius Age overlaps it from the year 1638 and will continue until the year 4212.

The Age of the Pisces belongs to the Zodiac's variable signs, so it always starts with goodwill and ends with madness and self-destruction. During the Pisces Age, the three main religions: Christianity, Judaism, and Islam expanded and were blown out of proportion, using extreme control, threats and intimidations by dictating to their followers:

▪ Stating they must arrive to prayer complexes and religious classes, setting dates of holidays and ceremonies.

▪ Prohibiting the mix between believers from different religions; especially when it comes to marriage or burial, then it gets even more absurd, declaring that marriage ceremonies may only unite those who believe in the same religion or mandating that burial ceremonies only allow 'their believers' to be buried on 'their land'.

▪ Asserting what and when to eat, on which days to strike and fast.

▪ Receiving donations up to the establishment of cults or radical factions.

● **All religions work in the form of unnecessary mediation agencies** between humans and *The Creation* (God) while they have been funded by governments, the public, and generations of believers.

● **Between all religions there is a consistent marketing competition** that promises to unite their believers and transform them to 'better people' by giving them answers from the 'holy' books, which mostly contain tales from ancient times, remember:

● **Material will never be holy - except the spirit of souls.**

● **The industrial-religion is and has been rolling tons of money** for generations by the exploitation and servitude of their believers into slaves in 'the name of God'.

• **Human beings have an ego; therefore, religions will not be able to exist in peace.** Historical evidence: religions have never united but divided and dispersed hatred up to the extinction of all that is different and unfortunately, it's also relevant even today.

*Religion goes against human freedom of choice. In the universe, there is **no religion – but only faith.** It is the inner faith that makes the difference and not the external appearance. **In every aspect of life, the moment you ask 'why' and do not receive a logical answer, it is time to rethink the matter.***

"Around the world people pay their respects to glorify religious leaders clothed in various outfits.

Who is portrayed as more reliable and trustworthy than true people of the spirit, such as mystics and mediums who are portrayed as flighty, strange, or charlatans?

Person's outward appearance and clothing do not indicate his quality, integrity, reliability and true personality."

It is worth repeating this vital point, religions exist from the money of the government, donations, public and generations of believers. There is a constant marketing competition between religions which promises to bring their believers 'closer to God', to make them 'good' people, practicing reading from 'holy' books which were written by men from ancient times, in their language and point of view. Religious industries are making tons of money combining brainwashing and fear without innovation, turning the believers into 'slaves of religion'. It's crucial to repeat it again:

A religious man: deals with material: houses of worship, books, talismans, ceremonies, religious artifacts, and clothing.

A spiritual man: does not deal with religion or material but communicates with God / *The Creation* without any additional accessories, but with modesty and inner quiet.

There is no need for mediators to reach God. You are associated with *The Creation* by your very creation.

Human beings have egos - therefore religions cannot coexist in peace and this is proven historically:

religions have never united - they have divided and spread hatred to coercion, violated human freedom, exterminated the different, up to these days.

"There are no religions in the universe, but faith".

• **The material will never be holy - except for the soul. Religion is not spirituality.** Religion revolves around the matter and it's contrary to human freedom.

In the approaching Aquarius Age religions will be replaced by free faith.

As the level of education increases, religion will decline. Every new creation - requires chaos first!

• **Chaos** = Destruction for the purpose of a better new creation, as the following examples:

In order to renovate, to create order at home or anywhere - you must create **chaos:** make a mess and cleanup, arrange and organize until the desired order is created.

Creation of a planet requires **chaos** and the explosion of other planets - then a new planet will be created from their star-dust.

After the **chaos** of the Holocaust, the Jewish people were given the right to return from exile and establish a state in the Land of Israel otherwise, it would have never existed.

In order to wipe-out the religions, **chaos** must be created, as every new creation requires the destruction of the former.

The purpose of the universe:

You were created by the extraterrestrials / *The Creators* on Earth (which is used as a laboratory for experiments) for the purpose of creating human beings, and you (which were created) will create other human beings and so on, endlessly. Everything is made of a soul; you are a spirit embodied in a temporary body of matter.

The purpose of the spirit: to attest to its real nature and by that to testify to the nature of *The Creation.*

The purpose of the material: to continue the engine of *The Creation* through a technological-scientific-spiritual creation which progresses infinitely.

Here are some insights:

- **Do not take anything for granted.** There can't be a single truth. Continue to explore infinitely.

The Creation will never provide one final answer but will hide in order to allow a choice, to discover. If all was known, then there would be no point in the continuity of life. A mystery is permanent, this is the infinite motor of humanity.

- **The abundance is stabilizing and the lack is motivating.** It's adapted to all areas of life.

• **The number of souls in the universe is limited.** Every soul that comes in - requires another soul to leave, every birth requires the death of another.

The Creation will always allow humanity **freedom of choice** and if humanity approaches self-destruction, then *The Creation* will intervene to prevent it, as is happening today.

• **Humans will not be able to destroy Earth - only to destroy the temporary life on it.** The Earth lives billions of years and it does not need oxygen, water, soil, or natural resources to survive, yet humans, animals, and nature need them.

• **You were created** on Earth by the extraterrestrials / *The Creators*, in order to create human life, animals and nature, in order to attest to the nature of the spirit which is embodied in the matter.

• **The material cannot please the soul** for long, emotions are associated with the soul and not with the matter. All diseases originate from the soul.

• **It is not possible to heal a soul by means of material alone;** each person has the natural capability to heal his own soul and body by activating his DNA coils.

• **Everything lives and breathes around you** with resonance and frequency, both on Earth and in the universe where everything is connected and dependent on one another.

All the planets in the solar system are energetically linked, the movement of one - affects all the rest. So, destruction in one part of Earth - affects all parts of it and affects the stars of the solar system. Continued environmental destruction in one part - will cause natural disasters in other parts, as all souls in the universe are connected and impacted by one another.

On Earth, as well as the whole universe, **states of matter** can be changed, but never annihilated or destroyed.

• **You are an infinite soul.**
All souls belong to one soul that crashed in the Big Bang, dispersed in the universe and created life on one planet in every galaxy.

• **Nothing has been nor will be yours forever,** even your soul is not yours - but lent to you.

• **Every soul chooses to be embodied in a temporary body on a planet / Earth -** in order to testify to the nature of your spirit to *The Creation.*

• **You cannot die.**
Life has no beginning and no end. You are infinite souls and will not cease to exist.

The Material world

The soul as spirit chooses to be embodied in the following hierarchy of matter:

- ✓   Dust, stone.
- ✓   Plant.
- ✓   Animal.
- ✓   Human beings or form of extraterrestrial.
- ✓   Up to enlightenment in the living body.

The Spirit World

The soul ends its incarnations in a material world and according to the amount of enlightenment within it can rise above as:

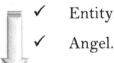

- ✓   Entity.
- ✓   Angel.
- ✓   Return to its original state as light and unite with *The Creation.*

At the time of death, each soul returns to its original state as *a spirit of light* and chooses without ego to reincarnate again as a soul or material. The soul can return thousands of incarnations to the point where it reaches enlightenment in a physical body.

The soul chooses to reincarnate in a body such as: dust, dirt, stone, plant, animal, human being, alien, light being, angel, etc. until it returns to its original source as light.

The amount of enlightenment within the soul is what enables the soul to rise from the material world to its place in the hierarchy of the spiritual world.

The entire universe is in the dark and there are only a few bright spots in the universe, the sun shines half a day to allow humanity to discover what already exists in darkness.

Every soul has a role in this world. After death, *The Creation* will never be angry or punish but will give compassion and love to all. Every soul can move up the spiritual hierarchy or go back to the physical hierarchy to correct its way.

About me

As a child, my parents were busy providing and I had a great deal of quality time by myself with an active imagination, patience with fearlessness of experiencing new things. At the age of six, I began to hear and see beyond and have conversations with deceased relatives. I noticed that when I asked a question - then a reply immediately popped into my mind with a vision. At the time, I thought that my experiences were typical to all children, but over the years I discovered that <u>I'm the weird one who is the exception.</u> Out of boredom and loneliness, I opened up to the world of the spirit, there I felt protected and there was no one to stop me or doubt my inner world.

Over the years, I completed my studies in architectural engineering and worked for many years in this field, yet I received a message that my real destiny is: to transfer messages, especially while the humanity is entering the Aquarius Age during my lifetime. As the years went by, I found out with the help of hypnosis that **I came from the future, from the year 3126, which is the middle of the Aquarius Age.**

I'm a spiritual woman, non-religious but full of endless faith in *The Creation* and *The Creators* because religion contradicts the human freedom of choice. I serve as a vessel for passing through messages and information.

Mystical events in my life

Realization of destiny

*D*uring my twenties, after many years of working as a practical architecture engineer, I decided to quit my job after receiving an inner message: *"My dear, it is time for you to go. The department is about to close down. This is the right time for you **to begin fulfilling your true destiny.**"* I shared this message with my manager, but despite his lack of faith a short time after I left - my prediction came true! This incident strengthened my sense of confidence to fulfill my destiny - working as a medium.

A messenger

I entered a restaurant and noticed an old man in tattered clothes looking-through the restaurant's window, it felt as if only I saw him. I went outside and put some money in his hand; he returned it back and said: *"I don't want your money; I want to eat."* He refused to come inside and stayed on the sidewalk. I bought him a meal and gave it to him. He kissed my palm and took it. On my way back inside I turned back to him but he vanished! He was a messenger who was sent to test me.

Encounter with extraterrestrials (Aliens)

O ne night I woke up and felt my entire body paralyzed except the blinking of my eyes. I saw two aliens standing in front of me, looking at me, their appearance was:

a bit taller than taller than a typical human, head shaped like an upturned pear, eyes large and cat-like, no eyelashes or body hair, small mouths, and noses. I wasn't afraid and began to communicate with them through telepathy: *"Why did it take you so long to come? I've been waiting for you since an early age."* They responded: *"We've been here all the time; **you are the one** who wasn't ready"*.

I remembered from that encounter how my body rose in the air and with a single blink they rotated me as I was floating in the air, so that I faced the floor and were led through my room's open window to a round spaceship covered with small illuminated windows with unusual structure of chains that made up the spaceship's floor. I received some kind of treatment in the spaceship, but they erased my memory afterwards. In that same night, I received the ability of x-ray vision, even remotely. In the following day, I woke up extremely tired. Over the years up to these days, I continue to communicate with them.

Trip to London

I went with a friend to London. We took a ferry at the River Thames. During that cruise, I closed my eyes and saw a vision: 'the entire city of London is on fire'. A few weeks later, I learned of *'The Great Fire of London'* that broke out in the year 1666! As we were celebrating my birthday, we went into a big toy store on Oxford Street. My friend announced to one of the salesmen that I'm a medium, to which he insisted to receive a personal message, so I told him: *"You were here in London at the age of 17 on a family trip with your parents and your little sister"*, he was stunned and said: *"It's true! How did you know that? I will gather the rest of the employees, please come to the fifth floor."*

Without requesting it, I found myself on the fifth-floor channeling voluntarily to the store's employees. In one special case, one manager approached me, so I asked him: *"Why are you sad? Your sister is already feeling better after her operation."* He was surprised and told me that his sister had undergone heart surgery. I began to see her heart from afar, using an 'x-ray vision': *"The source of your sister's heart condition was the lower left valve, which separates the chambers of the heart, it did not function properly and the problem was fixed".* Immediately, he called his mother who verified all the details were true!

After four hours we came out of the store and while we were standing on Oxford Street, I told my friend to look up at the sky: *"The Creation is sending us a message and a hug from above."* Shortly after, an airplane emerged and marked a white stripe in the sky.

The woman in black

One morning, a 70 years old woman came for a channeling session. She wore a black dress; her hair was black and disheveled. She sat in front of me and began to complain how mystics have 'ruined' her life by not allowing her to ever experience love or marriage.

I felt her negative energy and noticed a satanic male entity dwells within her, so I immediately protected myself and asked the entity within her: *"What have you come to me seeking? What is it that you want? I am protected, you cannot harm me."*

The woman continued complaining and began to curse, so I asked her to leave without paying. An hour later I smelled something burning in the room and when I lifted my head up, I saw a "fiery flame" erupting from the top of my head. I put out the fire; some burnt pieces of paper fell down but amazingly my hair and scalp weren't damaged. I immediately gathered the energy she sent me as a ball of fire and sent it back to her and I asked from *The Creation* to let justice be done.

Out of body experience

One night, I woke up from my sleep paralyzed without the ability to move, besides my eyes. On the wall in front of me, I saw a wide camera film open up and in it three picture frames. Paralyzed I saw myself in a form of a hovering white dove, flying between several images from my previous incarnations. My soul rose out of my chest and entered into the first picture frame. This process repeated itself three times.

In each frame I saw myself in different places, speaking a different language until the whole process ended. Moments later, a spiral white light appeared in front of me and it began to turn in a circle, while tiny chubby colorful angels, without any gender, were flying around the spiral and heavenly music of harp was in the background. Wow! That was a divine experience!

The prince of darkness / devil

I borrowed a spiritual book, read the first half, and agreed with almost everything written in it. In the following day, while reading the second half, I realized that the contents were not as "enlightened" as I had thought. I saw it as a moral obligation to note this in my first book, Divine Creation.

At midnight I placed the book on the nightstand and sunk into a deep sleep. Suddenly, I opened my eyes and couldn't move, aside from blinking, I lay on my side paralyzed and felt someone kneeling on my bed behind my back, pressure had been created in the mattress. Someone's elbow pressed into my right arm and I felt pain.

I saw that it was a male figure with a bull's head with thick glowing gold horns, which emerged from the upper part of his forehead. The pain in my right arm gradually intensified. I decided to speak with him voicelessly and politely asked him to leave and not bother me. I heard devious laughter from his throat. I summoned angels and entities to come and help me.

He applied force on my right arm, approached my right ear and whispered: *"Who do you think you are to dare write about me in your book, which will be published world-wide? You mustn't write what you've intended to nor slander my name. You are unaware of the fact that I have a respectable position in the universe in order to allow free choice to all. You shall never publish the name of the book you've read and if you do so - then I will visit you again... And while I'm here let's testify your force."*

He applied increased force on my right arm and that was so painful. Suddenly, I felt a "ball of light and fire" stirring in my belly and it reached my chest, entered my right arm which lifted up and pushed him away, he disappeared in an instant. I decided to share that encounter: **the devil does exist and has a place in the universe.**

I realized that good and evil do not exist. Maybe what's good for one person - is bad for the other. Everything is relative.

Everything exists around you in pairs:

Male and female; day and night;

darkness and light;

devil and angels; heaven and hell.

You even have been given the ability to lie,

because always telling the truth

will not enable you to choose.

All is done in order to balance

and allow you with free choice.

My mother's death

Six months before my mother's death, while she was still clear-minded, I had a dream in which my mother appeared alone in a room and told me:

"Hush.... don't tell anyone that I'm here. Only you can see me. They are asking me in Heaven to decide whether to stay here or to leave. What do you suggest I should decide?" I replied: *"Mother, I have no right to decide for you, that is a decision only you can make."* She replied back: *"O.K, I'll think what to do."* After that, I saw the number five.

Friday at four o'clock in the afternoon, I received a message to rush to the hospital. As I began driving toward the hospital, I felt that my mother was sitting in the passenger seat beside me. She said:

"I came to say goodbye. I chose to leave now, on a Friday afternoon when there is little traffic on the roads, because I know how much you hate traffic jams".

As I entered her room in the hospital at five o'clock, (as in my dream!) I found out that my mom passed away while I was driving. In the hospital room, I saw a vision in which she was standing, smiling, healthy, happy and suffering no pain while she entered *'The tunnel of light'.*

We are all made of souls; therefore, we cannot die, but only change form and keep on moving.

The soul is infinite. Each soul enters a host body - at the time of birth and exits it - at the time of death. Then, the soul transfers back to God, as a spirit. Each event that occurred in your lives **was meant to be - because you chose it!** *This is all to achieve personal empowerment, mature, complete cycles, and make a correction with your karma. You have received the most precious thing which no one else can give you and that is* **life - the only sacred thing.**

You cannot die.
You are an infinite soul that testifies itself
to The Creation / God,
by learning through being in
a temporary material body, when
all human actions testify to the nature of God.

Fear results from - the lack of knowledge.

Knowledge is power - which chases away fear.

If you know - then there is nothing to fear.

Chapter 1:
About the Ages

All my books were received by channeling. My first book, 'Divine Creation', contains insights and explanations about the purpose of humanity. In my second book, 'The Future' I predicted all the Ages of the 12 Zodiac Astrological, which directly affect humanity on Earth. There is no coincidence, every action has a hidden purpose, a divine pattern and an astrological-numerological cycle, when the Zodiac moves back from the order we are accustomed to in astrology, so after the Age of the Pisces, the Aquarius Age will begin.

Each Age lasts 2106 years.

Age-rays always begin 468 years before each age.

An Age: is associated with one of the 12 signs of the Zodiac and it's influenced by the age before and after it. Each age has positive and negative features which affect humanity on Earth: the environment, brotherhood, society, technology, sciences and more. Each new creation requires destruction of the previous.

Age-rays: As the Sun-rays appear before Sun-up, similarly the Age-rays rise and appear 468 years before the beginning of **each age.** In this way, there is always an overlapping period between ages toward the entry of the next Age and so on. The change will always be done through *chaos*, revolutions, wars, natural disasters, etc... The astrological Zodiac contains all 12 ages and affects the solar system.

"The beginning of every creation - requires chaos first."

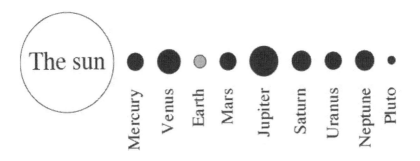

The Age-rays of the Pisces Age, which were aggressive and destructive, **began in the year 468 BC** when scientist Pythagoras became known as 'the father of number theory'. The Age of Pisces began in the year **0** (the birth of Jesus) and will continue into the Aquarius Age, up to the year 2106.

The Age-rays of the Aquarius Age began in 1638 AD, when Galileo Galilei, 'the founder of modern science' in the fields of physics, astronomy and mechanics, ridiculed religions and discovered that all planets surround the sun. The Aquarius Age will begin in the year 2106 and will continue up to the year 4212. (The Future, 2017).

The Ages cyclicality **moves backward** in the Zodiac:

From **Taurus** ➡ to **Aries** (& not to Gemini).

From **Aries** ➡ to **Pisces** (& not to Taurus).

From **Pisces** ➡ to **Aquarius** (& not to Aries).

From **Aquarius** ➡ to **Capricorn** (& not to Pisces)...

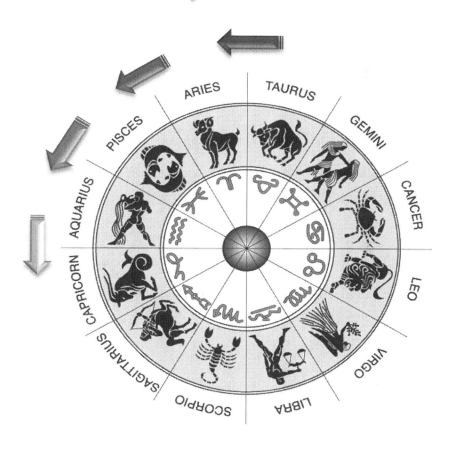

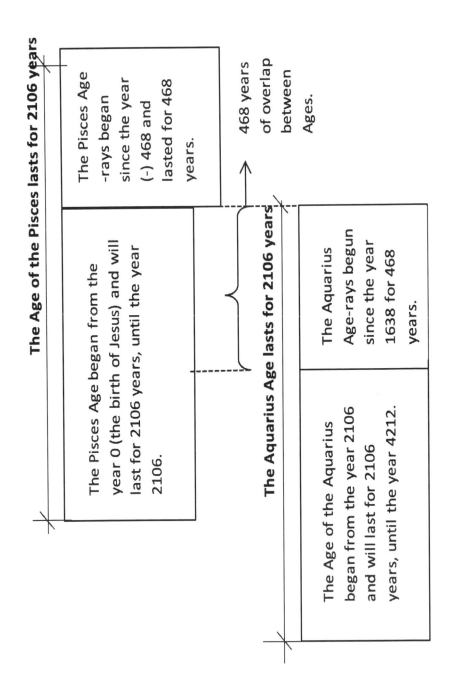

The Age of the Pisces lasts for 2106 years

The Pisces Age -rays began since the year (-) 468 and lasted for 468 years.

The Pisces Age began from the year 0 (the birth of Jesus) and will last for 2106 years, until the year 2106.

468 years of overlap between Ages.

The Aquarius Age lasts for 2106 years

The Aquarius Age-rays begun since the year 1638 for 468 years.

The Age of the Aquarius began from the year 2106 and will last for 2106 years, until the year 4212.

The beginning of the Age of the Pisces began in the year **0** with Jesus / Joshua, the God messenger, which had a significant role on a new order on Earth.

The Age of the Pisces = the Age of Man;

therefore, a male Jewish messenger ("You shall be a light unto the nations") was sent by *The Creation* to Earth, in order to abolish the religions and to open a new non-religion era without idolatry but faith.

Jesus preceded his time by an era, whereby absurdly and unintentionally he created the religion of Christianity. In the Age of Pisces, the three religions: Christianity, Judaism, and Islam - expanded into monstrous proportions. The double or two-sided Pisces sign (along with Libra and Gemini signs) always starts with a good will to help and goes on to power, control, extremes, madness, and self-destruction.

All religions are unnecessary "mediation agencies" between man and *The Creation* and are based on brainwashing and writing to their followers:

when to fast or set holidays, to defame and hate the other to the point of killing and annihilating the other. Circumcision, marriage, divorce, ritual purity, kashrut, conversion, etc... are determined and run with an old-fashioned opinion of religious clergy without freedom of choice, allowing only their believers to be buried in 'their land', set by hierarchy, favors and corruption, until the establishment of channels of communication, cults, extremist factions and all under the auspices of religion.

This reached up to an absurd reality: the establishment of the Vatican State!!

This is a Christian religious state that exists in Rome under the patronage of the Pope, while <u>the absurd is that the Romans themselves crucified and killed Jesus</u>!! Therefore, *The Creation* will permanently destroy the Vatican and none of them will remain alive. This is a biblical closure.

The Ages time tables

An Age: continues throughout **2106** years. Age-rays: appear **468** years before the beginning of each Age, it creates a gradually overlapping period between Ages.		
The Astrological Ages order	**The beginning of the Age Rays**	**The beginning of the Age**
The Age of Taurus	From the year **4680** BC Circle **9** - Cyclicality **2**	From the year **4212** BC Circle **9** - Cyclicality **2**
The Age of Aries	From the year **2574** BC Circle **4** - Cyclicality **6**	From the year **2106** BC Circle **4** - Cyclicality **6**
The Age of Pisces	From the year **468** BC Circle **7** - Cyclicality **9**	From the year **0** <u>Nativity of Jesus</u> Circle **7** - Cyclicality **9**

In the year **468** AD: the scientist Pythagoras was known as 'the father of the number theory and string theory'.

In the year **1638** AD: (**2106 - 468 = 1638**) the scientist Galileo Galilei discovered that light is **10** times faster than the sound, he also found that all the planets are surrounding the sun.

The Ages time tables

The Astrological Ages order	The beginning of the Age Rays	The beginning of the Age
The Age of Aquarius	From the year **1638** AD Circle **7** - Cyclicality **5**	From the year **2106** Circle **7** - Cyclicality **5**
The Age of Capricorn	From the year **3744** Circle **3** - Cyclicality **1**	From the year **4212** Circle **3** - Cyclicality **1**
The Age of Sagittarius	From the year **5850** Circle **8** - Cyclicality **6**	From the year **6318** Circle **8** - Cyclicality **6**
The Age of Scorpio	From the year **7956** Circle **5** - Cyclicality **3**	From the year **8424** Circle **5** - Cyclicality **3**
The Age of Libra	From the year **10,062** Circle **1** - Cyclicality **8**	From the year **10,530** Circle **1** - Cyclicality **8**
The Age of Virgo	From the year **12,168** Circle **6** - Cyclicality **4**	From the year **12,636** Circle **6** - Cyclicality **4**

The Ages time tables

The Astrological Ages order	The beginning of the Age Rays	The beginning of the Age
The Age of **Leo** An exceptional age.	From the year **14,274** Circle **2** - Cyclicality **9**	From the year **14,742** Circle **3** - Cyclicality **1**
The Age of **Cancer**	From the year **16,380** Circle **8** - Cyclicality **6**	From the year **16,848** Circle **8** - Cyclicality **6**
The Age of **Gemini.** Finish 12 cycles of the Zodiac.	From the year **18,486** Circle **4** - Cyclicality **2**	From the year **18,954** Circle **4** - Cyclicality **2**
The Age of **Taurus** A new Zodiac cyclicality.	From the year **20,592** Circle **9** - Cyclicality **7**	From the year **21,060** Circle **9** - Cyclicality **7**

∞ The Zodiac tables of the ages / 1 ∞

The Zodiac sign	An Age-Rays beginning			An age beginning			Numerological meaning
	From the year	circle	Cyclicality	From the year	circle	Cyclicality	
Taurus	4680 B.C	9	2	4212 B.C	9	2	Circle 9: Closure for a new beginning. Cyclicality 2: chaos, knowledge & ...
Aries	2574 B.C	4	6	2106 B.C	4	6	Circle 4: Order, development and strengthening. Cyclicality 6: Unity, commitment, knowledge and discoveries.
Pisces	468 B.C	7	9	0 Nativity of Jesus	7	9	Circle 7: Repair, inventions, knowledge and spiritual. Cyclicality 9: Closure for a new beginning.
Aquarius	1638	7	5	2106	7	5	Circle 7: Repair, inventions, knowledge and spiritual. Cyclicality 5: Changes, Justice and new order.

❧ The Zodiac tables of the ages / 2 ☙

The Zodiac sign	An Age-Rays beginning			An age beginning			Numerological meaning
	From the year	circle	Cyclicality	From the year	circle	Cyclicality	
Capricorn	3744	3	1	4212	3	1	**Circle 3:** Community, communication and plenty. **Cyclicality 1:** Beginnings, ideas and unity.
Sagittarius	5850	8	6	6318	8	6	**Circle 8:** Reorder, responsibility, strengthening. **Cyclicality 6:** Unity, commitment, knowledge and discoveries.
Scorpio	7956	5	3	8424	5	3	**Circle 5:** Changes, Justice and new order. **Cyclicality 3:** Community, communication and plenty.
Libra	10,062	1	8	10,530	1	8	**Circle 1:** Beginning, ideas and consolidation. **Cyclicality 8:** Reorder, responsibility, strengthening.

∞ The Zodiac tables of the ages / 3 ∞

The Zodiac sign	An Age-Rays beginning			An age beginning			Numerological meaning
	From the year	circle	Cyclicality	From the year	circle	Cyclicality	
Virgo	12,168	6	4	12,636	6	4	**Circle 6:** Unity, commitment, knowledge and discoveries. **Cyclicality 4:** Order, development and strengthening.
Leo An exceptional age	14,274	2	9	14,742	3	1	**Circle 2:** chaos, knowledge and communication. **Cyclicality 9:** Closure for a new beginning. *With circle 3: Community, communication and plenty.. **Cyclicality 1:** Beginnings, ideas and unity.
Cancer	16,380	8	6	16,848	8	6	**Circle 8:** Reorder, responsibility, strengthening. **Cyclicality 6:** Union, commitment and knowledge.

∞ The Zodiac tables of the ages / 4 ☊

The Zodiac sign	An Age-Rays beginning			An age beginning			Numerological meaning
	From the year	circle	Cyclicality	From the year	circle	Cyclicality	
Gemini	18,486	4	2	18,954	4	2	Circle 4: Order, development and strengthening. Cyclicality 2: chaos, knowledge and communication.
Taurus — A new round of the zodiac	20,592	9	7	21,060	9	7	Circle 9: Closure for a new beginning. Cyclicality 7: Repair, inventions, knowledge and spiritual.
Cosmic year	25,272	2	9	Every 25,272 years - One cosmic year passes.			Circle 2: chaos, knowledge and communication. Cyclicality 9: Closure for a new beginning.

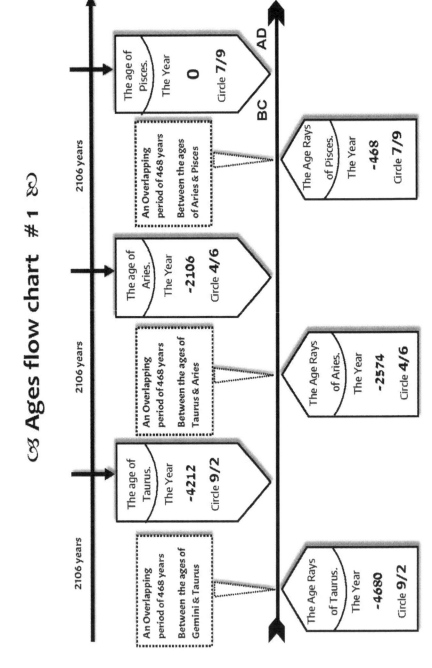

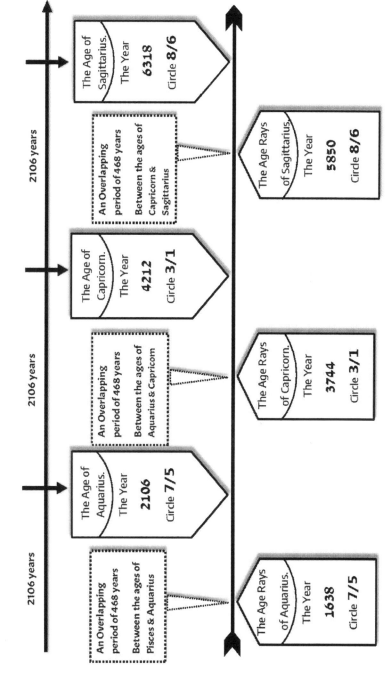

ॐ Ages flow chart #2 ॐ

2106 years — 2106 years — 2106 years

The Age of Sagittarius.
The Year
6318
Circle **8/6**

An Overlapping period of 468 years
Between the ages of Capricorn & Sagittarius

The Age Rays of Sagittarius.
The Year
5850
Circle **8/6**

The Age of Capricorn.
The Year
4212
Circle **3/1**

An Overlapping period of 468 years
Between the ages of Aquarius & Capricorn

The Age Rays of Capricorn.
The Year
3744
Circle **3/1**

The Age of Aquarius.
The Year
2106
Circle **7/5**

An Overlapping period of 468 years
Between the ages of Pisces & Aquarius

The Age Rays of Aquarius.
The Year
1638
Circle **7/5**

ᏮᏮ Ages flow chart #3 ᏮᏮ

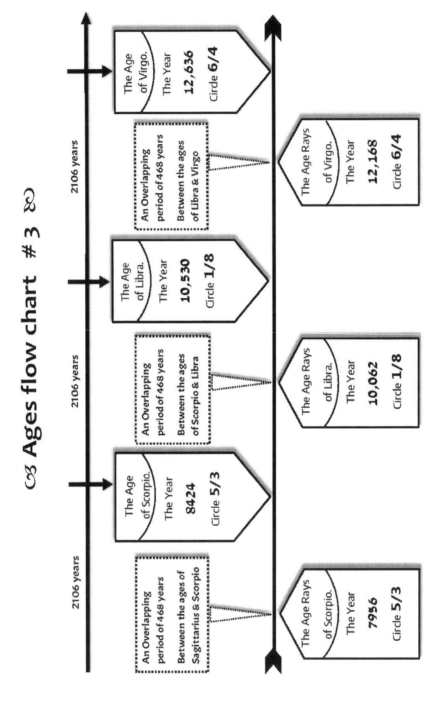

2106 years

The Age of Virgo.
The Year **12,636**
Circle **6/4**

The Age Rays of Virgo.
The Year **12,168**
Circle **6/4**

An Overlapping period of 468 years
Between the ages of Libra & Virgo

2106 years

The Age of Libra.
The Year **10,530**
Circle **1/8**

The Age Rays of Libra.
The Year **10,062**
Circle **1/8**

An Overlapping period of 468 years
Between the ages of Scorpio & Libra

2106 years

The Age of Scorpio.
The Year **8424**
Circle **5/3**

The Age Rays of Scorpio.
The Year **7956**
Circle **5/3**

An Overlapping period of 468 years
Between the ages of Sagittarius & Scorpio

ℭ Ages flow chart #4 ℘

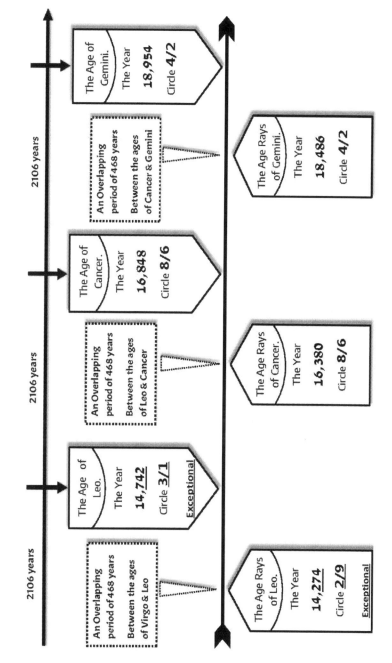

The Age of Gemini.
The Year **18,954**
Circle **4/2**

2106 years

An Overlapping period of 468 years
Between the ages of Cancer & Gemini

The Age Rays of Gemini.
The Year **18,486**
Circle **4/2**

The Age of Cancer.
The Year **16,848**
Circle **8/6**

2106 years

An Overlapping period of 468 years
Between the ages of Leo & Cancer

The Age Rays of Cancer.
The Year **16,380**
Circle **8/6**

The Age of Leo.
The Year **14,742**
Circle **3/1**
Exceptional

2106 years

An Overlapping period of 468 years
Between the ages of Virgo & Leo

The Age Rays of Leo.
The Year **14,274**
Circle **2/9**
Exceptional

∞ Ages flow chart #5 ∞

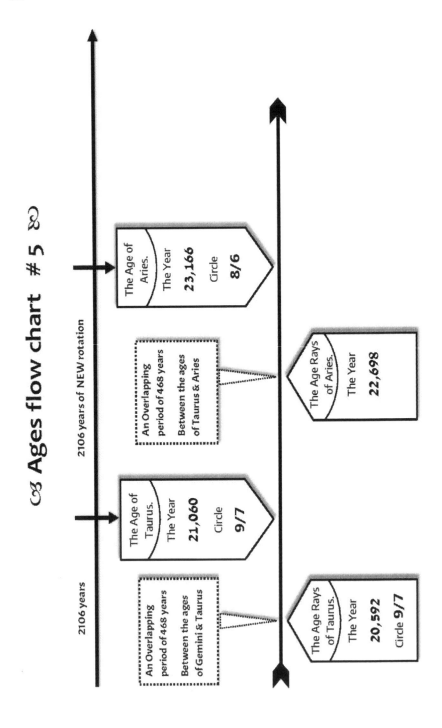

2106 years of NEW rotation

2106 years

The Age of Aries.
The Year **23,166**
Circle **8/6**

An Overlapping period of 468 years
Between the ages of Taurus & Aries

The Age Rays of Aries.
The Year **22,698**

The Age of Taurus.
The Year **21,060**
Circle **9/7**

An Overlapping period of 468 years
Between the ages of Gemini & Taurus

The Age Rays of Taurus.
The Year **20,592**
Circle **9/7**

Chapter 2:
The Age of the Pisces

It is important to mention the properties of the Age of the Pisces, from which we are separating in this period, in order to explain what is expected for humanity as we are entering the Aquarius Age in the year 2106:

Age-rays: began since the year 468 BC.

The beginning of the Age: commences at the year 0 AD, the birth of Jesus.

The end of the Age: with the entry of the Aquarius Age from the year 2106 AD.

Circle 7 - Cyclicality 9: (7) an age of spirituality, knowledge and inventions, introspection along with (9) chaos, wars, ending and starting a new beginning. **Therefore, during the Age of Pisces, the power and control of religions (7) will increase along with corruption in every aspect of life and must end with humongous world-wide chaos (9) of the old world, as we are witnessing now.** Hence, in order to predict the future, you must engage numerological and astrological signs and figures, as I provided this divine research in my second book, The Future / 2017.

The Age-rays are always begun in the year (-) 468 BC
Calculation: year (-) 468 = 468-0; 4 + 6 + 8 = 18 = 1 + 8 = 9

Each Age lasts for 2106 years and will end in year 2106 = 0 + 2106.

The sum of the Age digits or Age-rays is always 9 = completion and preparation for the new.

The Age of the Pisces belongs to the changing signs (among Libra and Gemini) always starts with good intentions yet with moods and destructive tendency.

The Pisces sign has the element of water and its planet is Neptune. This age embodies a paradox between spirituality, scientific discoveries and technological innovations along with power, control, and self-destruction.

The properties of the Age of the Pisces:

 Positive properties:

Education and aesthetics, compassion and empathy, creativity, sexuality, and spirituality.

 Negative properties:

Moods and schemes, power and control, vulnerability, stubbornness, and self-destruction.

Signs of the ending Age of Pisces:

The Age began in year (-) 468 BC: in this year, Pythagoras became famous as 'the father of number theory', he also claimed that the moon was rough and had mountains similar to those on Earth.

The year 0 AD - the birth of Jesus: *The Creation* sends Jesus as a high light entity to Earth in order to open a new age.

The mother of Jesus, the Virgin Mary symbolizes the complementary Virgo that is located opposite to the Pisces sign in the Zodiac.

The Age of the Pisces is the Age of Man and Jesus as a man was born to spread the gospel, he came to abolish the religions and unite humanity with free faith. **Jesus was a Jew prophet who preceded his time** (Jews: "You shall be a light unto the nations") and presented God as a collective entity and not as a source of fear but forgiveness and love, all coming from the same source regardless of religion, nationality, sex, or race.

Jesus pointed out that material achievements are marginal and that it is not right to invest in anything as short-lived as the body and matter but to invest in learning, thinking and creating, which will lead to discoveries, and advance humanity without studying religion, history and archeology as they deal and discuss the past without contributing anything to building humanity's future.

Only science will march humanity forward!

Multiple births, worshiping religions, rituals, and blind faith, deprive from people their freedom to choose for themselves, which is forbidden by *The Creation*.

All these create generations of slavery, economic burden on the society, being stuck in one place without renewal, which doesn't advance humanity scientifically and technologically.

Only fearless education, science, and rethinking will produce innovations. Technological-scientific and many developments will lead humanity to its destination, in order to create free and enlightened human beings, animals, and nature, which will become more advanced during the generations.

From the year 2016 until the year 2106 = 90 years = preparing the humanity for the Aquarius Age.

The Age of religions
Faith in material and control of religions

 The Age of the Pisces always starts well:

bringing new believers from a good place of helping others, giving and compassion, civil unions, community volunteering, religious jobs, building prayer houses: temples, churches, synagogues, mosques, and monasteries. Religions do not allow freedom of choice, otherwise, they will lose their power to control.

 And goes on to power and extremism:

religious coercion and persecution, forced conversion, religious orders, rigid religious laws, the killing of populations under the auspices of the Crescent and the Crusades, the Inquisition, the Holocaust, pogroms, massacres of peoples, tribes, and races.

Religions have competition regarding the size of the construction of prayer houses, to demonstrate their 'real power'. There are also brainwashing cults: Scientology in Christianity, Kabbalah in Judaism, Jihad in Islam, etc.

Religions are the longest-lasting mass scams.

Governments control their citizens with the divide and control method. Therefore, they encourage religions, which separate the population. Religions set for their believers guidelines, such as: getting to prayer sites, religious lessons, what and when to eat, what to wear, when to strike and fast, defamation of other religions and pagan rituals (such as: circumcision, marriage, divorce), funeral ceremonies that allow only their believers to be buried in their section of land and all who are different are ostracized. They also set hierarchy and corruption, receiving donations and benefits up to the establishment of religious media channels, cults, and factions.

Even **Kabbala** is not spirituality, but 'friendly and cohesive brainwashing', on the one hand it's unifying but is being managed like any other religion: by clergymen, setting procedures, laws, transferring lessons in a media channel and supported by donations from its followers. **Any material will never be holy except the spirit, the soul.**

'Holy books' were written in ancient times by man *"in the name of God"* and marketed by brainwashing to the masses by priests, rabbis, and imams who received public and government funds to build prayer sites. ***The Creation* does not want nor need humanity's worship. There is no need to recite verses, laws, prayers, and ceremonies, which are all considered idolatry!** *The Creation* (spirit) is not to be subjugated through matter (religions) but through inner free faith (spirit).

This is the insight that Jesus tried to send during his generation, that divinity is not in matter but in the spirit. He was crucified in order to control people and not to allow them to start thinking for themselves. How will the religious industry survive without public funds?

In the approaching Aquarius Age, the dominating **power of man will be replaced by female compassion,** the image of the woman will intensify and **Jesus will reappear in the form of many women who will bring news gospel to humanity.**

Once they dictate to you what 'to do and not to do', it is time to use your logic, because this is not spirituality.

The Creation will never act out of power and control over others but will allow free choice, equality, love, and compassion.

All people are born naked and equal, no one is above the other. Every religious person has been brainwashed and acted as a machine out of the 'herd effect', without free and modern thinking. People adopt a religious appearance and outward clothing, in order to feel 'purity' and belonging. *The Creation* sees this as lack of progress, lack of logic without self-choice, in external disguise dictated by a community as a herd, combining laws, rituals, and **glorifying the visible matter over invisible spirituality.**

All religions were invented by man. Since ancient times religions have been glorifying the man over the woman, out of fear of her.

The way to control others is to deny their rights! Human freedom must be allowed above all. There will never be a right to control others! This applies to human beings, animals, and nature.

Spirituality requires freedom; therefore, religions are not spiritual and will eventually be destroyed, while humanity is entering the Aquarius Age which officially begins in the year 2106.

In Hebrew, *Eloha* means a single God, and *Elohim* means many Gods. Jews refer to God as *Elohim*.

The Creation always gives you a choice from at least two options, therefore God can never be one, in order to allow you to choose.

Divine Creation = the cosmos duplicates itself forever.

The sign of Pisces: Water
Liquid-based inventions

 The Age of the Pisces always starts well:

in this age, transportations that float on the water were created and people learned how to turn water into energy, such as: sailing boats and ships on the water, water mills, and dams. The techniques for marine transportation (liquid), the construction of rowing boats, steam-powered boats, diesel engines, and electricity have been improved.

It also included the pumping of fluids and fossils from the Earth's soil and turning them into fuel (liquid) for world-wide transportation. Maritime traffic opened the period of discoveries, connected people across the globe, opened the economic and trade market between countries and helped mix cultures between countries. This movement continues to this day world-wide.

From the year 1440, sailors from the European continent, such as: Marco Polo, Christopher Columbus, Vespucci Amargo, Vasco da Gama, Captain Cook, and others, sailed around the globe and brought the world's citizens together by exchanging trade between continents, transporting people, and goods.

This mixing of world-wide cultures continues to this day and unites humanity, contributes to commercial competition which reduces prices and increases the variety of produce and merchandise available, with open world-wide trade, fast and cheap, everyone can trade without limitations. These moves will develop further in the approaching Aquarius Age, a great future in front of us.

Since 1638, with the arrival of the Aquarius Age-rays, we can notice a combination of the signs of Pisces (water) with Aquarius (air) as pressure pumps which push water by pressure, fountains, sprinklers and pipes for rainwater, drinking and irrigation, construction of dams, and pneumatic pumps by air pressure. See hydraulic pump diagram from 1728:

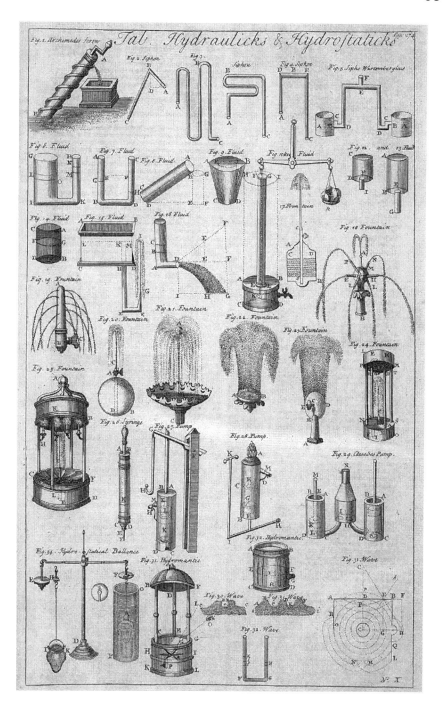

And goes on to power and extremism:

the sign of Pisces loves power, control and money, this is expressed in building wooden ships for discovering countries and the need to conquer. These ships transport people, food, spices along with weapons, mortars, and cannons; even up to building huge ships, such as: cargo ships, yachts, pleasure ships, containers, destroyers and submarines with weapons, bombs and warplanes, and unfortunately human trafficking and illegal drugs.

A huge shortage of drinking water

As we separate from the Age of the Pisces, which symbolized water, similarly, we observe the signs that we are 'separating from water' = lack of drinking water.

In the Aquarius Age, there will be a huge shortage of drinking water. This fact is absurd when it comes to Earth which contains mostly water.

Desalination and sewage treatment methods for reusable wastewater will be constructed in public and domestic facilities.

The Age of Man
The wars of the male ego

 The Age of the Pisces always starts well:

a male leader who unites and cares about his family and his citizens. It's the Age of romance, expression of feelings and love, in poetry, writing in public.

The woman is supported by a man who has to support her and their descendants.

 And goes on to power and extremism:

in the Age of the Pisces, man ruled: masters and servants, nobles, kingdoms and princes, dynasties and palaces, emperors and sheikhs, classes and aristocracy, battles, wars and conquests, empire-making, businessmen, tycoons, rich men and oligarchs.

Men were allowed to marry many women, conquest and loot property, and impose heavy taxes on civilians. Slavery, inequality, rights and violation of human freedom also took place. They built luxury houses, castles, palaces, and estates.

It is an era of unjust division and the accumulation of large sums of money for individuals without regard to the economic situation of the community; an era saturated with killing and domination of millions by kings, generals, rulers, tyrants, leaders, kingdoms, emperors, and prime ministers, such as:

the empire of China and Japan, the Ottoman Empire, Napoleon, Alexander the Great, Mussolini, Stalin, and Hitler. The Arab states are always ruled by tyrants like Saddam Hussein, Gaddafi, Mubarak, Asad, etc... All governments of the world will collapse during the Aquarius Age and a single world-wide female leadership.

The Age of the Pisces is characterized by a masculine Age of ego, power and control over matter and money: rich and wealthy, establishment of stock market, banks, investment houses and insurance companies that exist and are supported by public funds and mass of customers, using the casino method of customers financing each other whereby those who have monetary balance pay for those who are in debt.

In the middle, the financial institutions charge interest, offer loans and produce sustained economic slavery for generations by creating a repeated financial dependence.

As we are entering the Aquarius Age towards the year 2106, all the unnecessary will collapse and disappear thanks to the power of the masses, the world's citizens, so all these institutions are unnecessary and will collapse and disappear for the sake of a simple easy life, without financial dependence, a monetary alternative in providing valuable assistance, known as barter and commercial trades. Human freedom and justice will dictate moves from now on.

The processes will become accelerated until the beginning of the Aquarius Age in the year 2106, the age of justice and truth, order will be made only by the citizens, all the unnecessary will disappear, exposing corruption in every field, **justice will be done with each one, when every self-action will come back to each person during his life.** The Aquarius Age will benefit all citizens, no longer the power of individuals but of the masses, through world-wide civil revolutions, because **"The beginning of each creation - requires chaos first".**

In the upcoming Age of Pisces, man ruled and led to death and destruction. In the coming Aquarius Age, the woman will rise up in the world and will march the humanity to ban the destruction, the killing, and the wars; this will lead to a better world full of compassion, love, and brotherhood, technological and communication union, integration and unification of cultures, world peace under world-wide females.

In the Age of the Pisces, the man controlled and empowered himself with privileges to control; he was able to acquire / marry a number of women which he kept as his private property and to reduce the status and rights of the woman, especially when the male clerics ruled, restricted, established laws and wrote "holy books" in their language, within their culture. They desired to control others, mainly the woman, lest "she" rebel because they were afraid of her power.

It is well known that the easiest way to control the masses out of rebellion, is through the use of force, instilling fears, laws, regulations, supervision, punishments and arrests (as is currently done in Syria, China, North Korea, etc.).

Towards the end of the Pisces Age, as we are entering now the Aquarius Age, which will start in the year 2106, *The Creation* creates chaos of male extreme control by dictators, rulers and corrupt public figures who will abuse the lives of others, abolish and rule out laws and human rights, all in order to wake-up the citizens out of sleep and restore the power back to the masses.

World-wide civil revolutions will shift the power from individual control to communal and cooperative leadership. Earth's frequencies are changing in order to prepare humanity for the coming of the Aquarius Age. Governments will be abolished and instead of them: The People's Council will be established with direct access to citizens.

Remember: as we are entering the Aquarius Age, justice will be done with each one, in which every self- action will come back to each person during his life. Towards the beginning of the Aquarius Age, **a great insight will enter and affect Earth's citizens.**

There is a world-wide agenda for all the citizens of the world who seek the same conditions from their governments. Multiple governments are unnecessary and not economic. Multiple governments limit and create borders between countries, which does not allow the world's citizens to move freely. In the Aquarius Age, there won't be any borders between countries, the citizens will be able to move and live in any country they request without visas, a world without wars.

Earth will become a paradise! The Earth belongs to all living on it, no one has the right to own part of it. You are all guests for a short time on this planet and you don't have the permission to claim anything to yourselves from the lands, water, air, and natural resources, nor to imprison animals, eat animals, experiment on animals, disrupt climate, and destroy life and nature.

"Whatever you create - comes back to you".

Age of enlightenment and science
Rigorous study methods

 The Age of the Pisces always starts well:

the establishment of educational institutions for general education and high-education, the study of languages, technologies, training people, and enriching them with knowledge. Virgo is complementary to the Pisces sign in the Zodiac, therefore, in the Age of the Pisces, there is an acceleration in the fields of science, discovery, inventions, high-education, science, universities and colleges.

From the year 1638, the Aquarius Age-rays shined on Earth, so in the last 400 years the Aquarius Age has **merged and then pushed the science and inventions forward:**

1490: explorers discovered countries.

1500: the invention of printing and electricity.

1760: the Industrial Revolution.

1969: the theory of relativity, research and discoveries, inventions and patents, research institutes, computers and robotics, the entering of science into home appliances, and media that connects the world's citizens.

Since the 1980s: advanced and biological medicine, medical devices that prolong life, esthetic surgeries, robotic organs, organ transplantation, and pacemakers. Improvement in the fields of aviation, satellites, space flights and more.

The Pisces sign adores knowledge and studies, and because of its location in front of the Virgo sign in the Zodiac, these effects have enriched in the last 500 years the progress and knowledge, inventions and technology, high-education institutions, universities, colleges, and organizations. All of this is in order to march humanity forward, to narrow the gap between us and our *Creators* in order to meet with them during the Aquarius Age.

In the Zodiac, because the Pisces sign is in front of the Virgo sign (knowledge and inventions) and is combined with the fast Aquarius sign (that entered since the year 1638), technology and communications began to advance rapidly. Technological developments will continue to accelerate in order to prepare humanity for the official entry of the Aquarius Age starting in the year 2106.

 And goes on to power and extremism:

at the beginning of the Aquarius Age, human rights were not equally granted to citizens, children were employed in various jobs without the possibility of acquiring an education and were even forced to marry at an early age with the help of laws and regulations. Women struggled and received voting rights only approximately 100 years ago, along with them workers began to raise their voice and to receive rights.

Death sentences, field trials, guillotines, and body parts were part of the ancient law. Then came strict methods of study with punishments, whipping, including isolation and denouncement of the other until the establishment of institutions for "disturbed" children / juvenile prisons and facilities of people with mental disorders.

The Pisces sign is known for its tendency to resemble others. On the positive side it spurs itself to copy, improve and bypass the other, so it creates itself every time anew. However, on the negative side, it encourages people to unnecessary competitions, envy, and the obsessive need to resemble others.

The Age of the Pisces determines rules of adaptation in the fields of life and education for the entire population as if they were all the same, and all the 'exceptions' are sent to the 'diagnostician' professionals who authorized themselves to diagnose without any required spiritual capacity (such as a medium capable of seeing beyond the physical body of the human incarnations, Karma, and frequency).

These children and adults are mistakenly diagnosed and sent to talk with psychologists and from there to psychiatrists for prescription medicines, as they must 'adapt themselves to the rest', so they will not interfere with **the old fashion school system that no longer fits the new age.** This is done in order to harm the self-confidence of these children and adults, make them waste money, become addicted and enrich the pharmaceutical companies.

Here is an example of the impact of science on critical Earth movements:

thanks to the chaos of World War II, *The Creation* gave the necessary knowledge to mathematician Alan Turing to crack the Enigma-code, to discover the German plans, in order to end the war and to save human life.

Another example of the influence of science on that destructive Age of the Pisces of Man:

the nuclear theory basis began with Einstein and was carried out in practice by the American scientist Robert Oppenheimer: the production of two atomic bombs which were dropped on Hiroshima and Nagasaki in Japan and caused hundreds of thousands of deaths and wounded. **The Creation (God) will never allow humans or their Creators to destroy planet Earth.**

New Age Children

In order to bring new upgraded souls to Earth, other souls must leave because the number of souls in the universe is limited. **Every soul that enters a body at the time of birth - requires that another soul leave a body at the time of death. "The beginning of each creation - requires chaos first" We are all recycled souls of *The Creation* / God.**

The Creation decided to create chaos using corrupted satanic people and produce World War I which created World War II, with the aim of creating destruction and killing millions in order to free souls and bring in upgraded souls instead.

Since the year 1945, high and upgraded souls of Crystal and Indigo children have entered Earth. These are souls with compassion, love, caring and healing for people and the environment with a tendency to rebel, to do justice and to create chaos in order to create a world-wide change for the benefit of humanity. These are the wonderful children with "ADHD" who have come to:

• Protect, heal, and correct the existing reality with sharp frequencies and senses, they are curious, opinionated, sensitive, and attentive to the environment, so they are able to listen to whatever happens in their immediate and distant surroundings.

• Teach humanity about compassion, caring, and tolerance.

• Change and dismantle the world education system, to throw out the old and create a new system, to combine advanced teaching methods and advanced technologies with tolerance without grades, competition, penalties, and stiffness. An open learning environment that encourages new thinking, self-creation, and practical community learning, such as "Do not tell me - but show me".

Children with "ADHD" are divided into indigo and crystal:

Indigo children

Are high souls who have come from distant planets to help and advance technology scientifically and inventively for the benefit of humanity.

They are geniuses, inventors, competitive, sensitive, caring and sometimes even aggressive, all in order to reveal and change. They have a brilliant engineering and analytical mind in a variety of fields, such as: hi-tech, technology, science and medicine, aviation, commerce, and economics. These Children mostly do not find a common language with others and therefore, they came to Earth to learn for themselves how to communicate with people and to teach others how to reach to the environment.

Since the 1960s, indigo children accelerated science and technology, such as Steve Jobs (Apple), who was indigo & was born in the year 1955 (since the year 1945 a new period has started with fast technology and development). *The Creation* gave scientists the knowledge to advance humanity, develop computer systems, software, and hardware such as was done by Microsoft, Apple, Intel, IBM, Pioneer, Sharp, Panasonic, Toshiba, Hitachi, and others.

This led to the upgrading of living conditions, technological devices, setting up the Internet, e-mail, social networks, sites, and search engines. The following were also put in place: GPS, infrastructure of landlines and cellular telephone networks, satellite products, and many others.

Crystal children

After the environmental destruction (through the Industrial Revolution and World Wars), caused by corrupted satanic man. *The Creation* decided to bring into Earth the high souls of crystal children (with "ADHD"), just as the crystal is transparent and does not hide so are they: real and honest, fighting for the truth, making justice and order. They are souls full of curiosity, stubbornness and rebelliousness, impatience, love, and compassion.

They have a moral conscience not to harm but to benefit, are lovers and honor the nature, animals, music, and freedom. They prefer the outdoor instead of the indoor (classes and offices), were sent to Earth to protect, heal, repair the environmental destruction, develop new thinking, unite humanity, delete boundaries and limitations, change the outdated education system of the world, and connect people to emotions and consciousness. Here are some examples of the Crystal Children's activities:

The youth of the 1960s: if we add 20 years to 1945 = we will receive the crystal & indigo children, who brought to the world the slogan "Make peace, not wars". These movements expanded over the years:

• 'Greenpeace' activists: rescuing animals and natural resources in the sea and on land, by discovering and spreading the truth in world consciousness.

• Activist movements and organizations: discovering the truth and distributing it on the internet, such as Wikileaks, because knowledge is power.

• The citizens of the world express their opinion on social networks, unite and will create civil revolutions. These are the signs of the coming of the Aquarius Age which will officially starts in the year 2106.

Development of art and culture
Design, aesthetics, and consumerism

 The Age of the Pisces always starts well:

this Age is known for its love of culture and the arts, led to creativity, especially from the Renaissance, from the 14th century to the 17th century, until today. All were influenced by the entry of the Aquarius Age-rays since the year 1638.

Examples of this love of culture and the arts are painting, sculpture, literature, plastic arts, establishment of museums, exhibitions, performances, opera, music, dance, and more. It's the Golden Age of Engineering, architecture and interior design, science, medicine and aesthetics, consumerism, design, fashion, hair, accessories, body care, improved hygiene, understanding of viruses, bacteria, sports.

Health and beauty treatments included: spas, massage, acupuncture and laser therapy techniques. It's also the Age of water / liquid: pools, baths, saunas, Jacuzzis, oils, and creams.

 And goes on to power and extremism:

in the fields of art and culture, there are also characteristics of power, competitiveness, a delegation of authority and social classes based on the level of money, family belonging, wealth and celebrities whom create a contemporary culture and earn huge amounts of money as artists, actors, singers, athletes, and designers. During this period, there is a need for people to be famous and rich without the need for education, but stupidity and emptiness.

Any action that becomes extreme is considered wrong when people deal with purchasing matter, instead of expanding their knowledge and creating new insights and knowledge for the benefit of the next generation. Extremism has developed mainly in women, in areas such as: eating and mental disorders (bulimia and anorexia), starvation, self-hatred, photoshop, cosmetic surgery, Botox injections, minimizing the size of the clothes for the entire population, tattoos and body piercing, fitness centers and bodybuilding. There are even beauty contests, sports and diet plans combined with nutritional supplements, powders, fasting, home fitness equipment, and more.

This world-class false industry, which makes a fortune and does not benefit humanity, sets a standard that cannot be attained naturally but artificially and tempts people to resemble others who are considered "normal and happy", which causes problems with self-image.

When we look back 100 - 400 years, we find out that people did not engage in sports, bodybuilding, running, diet and beauty surgeries. In the East, we find that sports activity is moderate, such as: Chi-Kong, Taiichi, and Yoga. Life expectancy was short in the past. However, it had nothing to do with "lack of sports" but with the rise in hygiene and the improvement of science.

Active sports produce physical damage over time. Running erodes the bones of the body. Prolonged bicycle riding causes damage to fertility areas. It's better to drink warm water than cold water, which contracts internal organs.

The adapted sport to human beings is the relaxed sport, such as Yoga, Meditation, Chi-kung, Taiichi and many oriental teachings, which improves life. Any passive activity that makes the person happy - produces a frequency of health in his body (except for active sports which cause long-term damage). Remember that human beings were created similar to their *Creators* (the aliens and the gorillas), which also do not engage in dynamic physical activities.

With the arrival of the Aquarius Age, we will experience "a return to the past", relaxed sports activities, use of natural biodegradable or recycled products and agricultural products, without chemicals and pollutants.

The recycle revolution will force citizens to design and sew their own clothes, there will be community fashion, including vintage, second-hand, and most of the clothing will be made of breathing cotton with mostly light colors. The power moves from the rich fashion designers to the modest power of the masses.

We will be accepting and respecting of others, (without the need to love everyone) and will admire the highly educated and intellectual figures who contribute to the improvement and advancement of humanity. It will be the end of the Age of stupidity and the beginning of the Age of wisdom.

Competitive sports
Competitions, prizes, and ego glorification

 The Age of the Pisces always starts well:

a culture of physical and mental health. Competitions are designed to unite, inspire, and bring people together.

 And goes on to power and extremism:

throughout the Age of the Pisces, which enjoys studies, titles, contests, money, and ego, an industry of achievements and competitions has developed in a variety of fields such as sport, beauty, music, theater, stage, performance, art and exhibition. These have blossomed to the point that only certain people 'Can allow themselves' to participate in them. Who determines who is competent and who is not? Everything is based on personal taste.

Humans compete with each other for the foolish purpose of overcoming each other, they waste time and effort in order to 'win', but who do they win exactly?

Sports / Olympic competitions – Who are these people who set the rules and the score that forces all participants to line up, in order to overcome the results of other competitors? (instead of being creative, groundbreaking, and original). Which judge has the right to place his own personal taste as a rule? There are many types of sports in order to satisfy different tastes.

Music competitions - Who decides which music or songs sound pleasant to the ear? Which judge has the right to place his own personal taste as a rule? There are many types of music in order to satisfy different tastes.

Food competitions - Who decides what tastes good or smells better and what does not? Which judge has the right to place his own personal taste as a rule? There are many types of food in order to satisfy different tastes.

Fashion, beauty and interior design competitions Who determines what is beautiful, with good taste, and what is not? Which judge has the right to place his own personal taste as a rule? There are many types of fashion, beauty, and interior design in order to satisfy different tastes.

These competitions are forcing the participants to adapt themselves to the demands of contemporary style, determined by individuals! They do everything to 'win', rather than being themselves, creative, and talented, with their own looks, insights, and opinions. We are all guests here for a moment, who will remember if you were fat, thin, or beautiful? **Yet you will be remembered for which insights and contributions you left behind.**

Competitions do not contribute to the advancement of humanity but to the glorification of human ego and blind admiration. They create discrimination between a 'winner' and a 'loser'. Awards and losses lead to separation and division between people and create preference and admiration of one person over another. Therefore, all competitions are illogical and unnecessary.

The right way is to create a gathering partnership for everyone, to unite people in conferences, festivals, games, and programs where anyone can participate without restriction, in which anyone can display his talent, accept the other as he is without having to change or compete with him. Each person has a talent!

Feeding the masses
Eating animals and non-nutritious foods

 The Age of the Pisces always starts well:

the man was created from a hybrid between an alien and a gorilla, with differences in the percentage of DNA level, so three kinds of people were created, as I explained in my first book (Divine Creation / 2016):

- **The Asian man** was created at first (in Japan) - a mix with a low percentage of DNA from a male gorilla and high percentage of DNA from a female alien.

- **The black man** was created second (in Africa) – a mix with a high percentage of DNA from a male gorilla and a low percentage of DNA from a female alien.

- **The white man** was created third (in Europe) – a mix with an equal DNA percentage from a male gorilla and a female alien.

The gorilla feeds on plants, leaves, roots, fruits and sometimes insects and the food of the alien / extraterrestrial is essentially not material, but energy. The man was created as a vegetarian and became a meat-eater with fangs for survival in periods of drought in agriculture, and since then the human DNA has been disrupted and has shortened the human lives.

Since the beginning of the Age of the Pisces, agriculture was organic with self-growing, so farms contained organic products rich in fiber and fat. The combination of the Pisces sign (health) and the Aquarius sign (art) Ages brought the cookbooks from about 100 years ago.

And goes on to power and extremism:

with population growth and the need for world-wide feeding, the Age of the Pisces uses manipulations in order to increase the financial profit at the expense of the health of consumers by taking out the fiber and animal fat from the food and replacing it with cheap corn products and low-cost substitutes, such as white flour, white sugar, and non-animal saturated fat, and using toxic pesticides, watering agricultural crops in sewage water, without taking into consideration the future human damage.

It continues with the massive breeding of animals for slaughter and the introduction of hormones and additives to their bodies to enrich their flesh or for experiments on animals. Throwing live chicks into the trash, injecting hormones and constantly fertilizing cows in order to produce huge amounts of milk. Only pregnant cows can yield milk, and therefore cows are artificially constantly pregnant for most of their lives, producing unhealthy milk full of hormones. Humans are part of the animal world, in which animals only consume motherly milk from the same species. Mixing DNA between animals (mixing motherly milk or eating other animals) causes diseases in the long run. The calf is taken from its mother cow for the purpose of consuming its meat, which has led to the creation of multiple slaughterhouses and chicken cages.

Everything around you contains souls: humans, animals, plants, soils, and air. It is forbidden to abuse souls because everything returns to the sender. The person who abuses the soul creates circular karma that will return to attack him during his lifetime on Earth and his soul's incarnations.

In a short time of the past 100 years, in order to feed billions of people and mostly to earn money, humanity has undergone a destructive change, such as chemical spraying and pesticides, the use of hormones, massive growing of cattle farms and giant chicken coops, artificial fish ponds, industrialized fast and cheap food, lacking nutritional values, nutrition-less carbohydrates from fibers, foods high in sugar and substitutes that cause increased eating consumption and obesity.

The use of hormones, which are being introduced into food, animals, and medicine, such as steroids, birth-control, fertility, and intrauterine devices, causes a disruption of the thyroid function which leads to a variety of phenomena, including world-wide obesity.

Vast amounts of food are being dumped into the garbage, half the world is living in abundance and wastefulness, while the other half in poverty and starvation.

All that disrupts the person's food frequency and his DNA coils. It is causing an epidemic of hormonal and endocrine diseases, diabetes, heart, and various types of cancer, and diseases that will continue to kill millions worldwide.

As we enter the Aquarius Age, the Corrective Age, we will see a 'balance and health revolution', in which the number of diseases will be reduced, people will balance their lives with meditation, self-grown and bartered healthy food, biological and friendly pesticides, advanced alien and frequency technology devices.

During these days, *The Creation* brings insights to the world's citizens, reveals the truth, and brings new justice and order, as the symbols of the Aquarius Age, such as the return to vegetarian / vegan eating, the agricultural growing with non-chemical spraying as biological or organic pest control, and the eating of animals will be prohibited.

In every aspect of life, the power transfers from the control of corrupt individuals and families, to the control of civilian, in which the masses act with knowledge-sharing and justice.

The power of citizens will rise, their voices will be heard throughout the social media, and will lead to world-wide civil revolutions which will crush the injustices and world corruption towards a healthy better future.

The environment pollution
Destruction and depletion of natural resources

 The Age of the Pisces always starts well:

the Age of the Pisces commences with preserving natural reserves, cultivating the land with animals and manual labor, using natural tools, recycling, preserving and respecting plant and animal life, hybridizing crops and inventing new varieties of fruits and vegetables.

 And goes on to power and extremism:

in the last 100 years, since the Industrial Revolution, man has caused widespread environmental destruction, mainly by burning coal which produces carbon dioxide which traps heat in the atmosphere, spraying chemicals, capturing animals in zoos and circuses, breeding herds, chickens, eggs, and fish-ponds in huge masses, killing whales and dolphins, who are in the depths of the oceans and are entrusted with keeping Earth's secret code. Whoever hurts them will get impacted. Japan suffers from natural disasters, due to their hunting of whales.

The sun's rays hit the Earth and are returned to the atmosphere, causing an increase in the concentration of gases in the atmosphere (from coal combustion and gas emissions) which yields to less sunlight returning to space and thus accumulates in the atmosphere.

"The beginning of each creation requires chaos first". The Aquarius Age begins in the year 2106 and is meant to remove all that is harmful and destructive. The Earth shakes off all pollutants in order to renew itself and reminds humanity through the forces of nature, that for billions of years of existence nothing has destroyed Earth.

Empires and glorious kingdoms have come and gone, just like you are a guest for a moment on Earth. Destruction of the air, water, and soil reservoirs will never affect the existence and survival of the Earth but will affect only the entire living population that inhabits Earth temporarily.

Earth's frequencies change and refine in anticipation of the arrival of the Aquarius Age. The power of the world's citizens will take care of the well-being of humanity, as a result of which world-wide laws will be passed to reduce air, land and sea pollution and protect all the surrounding nature.

Every new creation requires chaos. The signs of the end of the Pisces Age (water) are the melting glaciers, rising water, and flooding. Luckily for us, the Aquarius Age is coming to the rescue of humanity.

Power, money, and corruption
Accumulation of individuals' money

 The Age of the Pisces always starts well:

it knows how to leverage, give help, strengthen others, create movement, and shorten processes.

 And goes on to power and extremism:

the sign of the Pisces is one of the Zodiac's "pair" signs, such as Gemini and Libra, which are characterized with changing moods, starting with good will, giving to the community and turns into control, self-destruction, and materialism. Material (money) will always be associated with a negative dimension of power and control.

The man dominated during the Age of the Pisces and caused environmental damage out of ego, narcissism, power, money, and status. From an egoistic survival need, the man rules through manipulations and corruption.

This can be seen today in politics, rulers, kings, generals, dictators, prime ministers, government officials, business owners, managers of companies, bankers and insurance companies and real estate agents, gangsters, managers of the criminal world, pimps, drug barons, cults, religious and "spiritual" leaders, corrupt men of law, all of whom are usually led by men and sometimes by powerful aggressive women.

In the Age of the Pisces, currency consists of material, banknotes, coins, credit cards, and loans. Money controls and causes citizens to take loans and be enslaved in debt slavery to financial institutions.

Towards the Aquarius Age, humanity will move to virtual currency and from there to world-wide internet trade without borders and limitations, in which the citizens of the world will trade by barter with each other.

The citizens of the world will create a new world and all that is corrupt will disappear. The money will collapse and with it the politicians, governments, banks, stock exchanges, insurance companies, pharmaceutical industry, fashion companies, malls, monarchs, wealthy corrupted people, and others.

How wonderful!
The power returns back to the masses!

Borders, languages, weapons, & vaccines

 The Age of the Pisces always starts well:

the sign of the Pisces is known for its love for studies and knowledge accumulation. Therefore, in this age, we will witness the blossoming and the rising of the languages, cultures, nations, and states.

 And goes on to power and extremism:

in the Age of the Pisces, men created the concept of **Divide and Conquer**, in order to control the population. Because of this, languages, religions, cultures, nations, countries, neighborhoods, and streets were created in order to make it easier for men to rule. Men fought, killed, destroyed, instilled fear, and prevented human freedom.

Borders

In the Age of Pisces, borders were established between countries and work visas are required.

Towards the Aquarius Age, borders between countries will be opened without the need for visas. Cities will be replaced with communities with the permission to enter only being granted to the members of the local community.

Languages

Each country has decided to adopt an identity (Divide and Conquer), such as a flag, language, dress, customs and cultures which distinguished them from the rest in order to preserve their 'identity'. In this way, many languages and cultures have been created in the world, which prevented people from understanding each other and uniting.

In the Aquarius Age, the official language of the world will be English, in order to enable unified and simple communication between the citizens.

Weapons

The Age of the Pisces adores ego and control. It goes along great with military power, in battles with horses, swords, knives, bows and arrows, through industrial and technological development of weapons, fighter planes, submarines, and bombs which were made in order to "protect territories" and fight against those who 'invaded' the borders.

In the Aquarius Age, citizens will be forced by law to return their weapons to the military, although there will be people who will resist. The army will be responsible to collect the weapons with the help of soldiers, military equipment, and robots. Women will bring world peace under a world-wide female leadership.

Vaccines

Approximately 100 years ago, the pharmaceutical industry began to vaccinate people, in order to reduce the population and destroy the natural immune system, to create generations of consumers of medicine and medical treatments.

Because of this, many babies, children, and adults have been affected by physical and medical issues of the nervous system, creating damages, such as cancer, diabetes, high blood pressure, autism, allergies, asthma, lactose, gluten, and flour intolerance, etc. All these diseases didn't exist prior to the vaccinations. The pharmaceutical industry still uses people as guinea pigs.

All vaccines contain toxic poisons which destroy the natural health and reduce life expectancy. All vaccines also damage quality of life, cause diseases, which lead people to become never-ending repeat consumers of the pharma industry's medicine and medical treatments. All this happens in order for the governments to be able to reduce the population, as the masses threatens their existence.

It is not the vaccines which have eliminated the most serious diseases from the world, but the high level of hygiene which has risen dramatically.

Medical drugs don't cure people completely, otherwise, people wouldn't need to continue consuming them over and over. Painkillers and psychiatric medicines are given by some doctors and psychiatrists, who think this is the solution. They are driven by their own financial well-being, and make patients become 'prisoners' as drug addicts.

Towards the Aquarius Age, there will be world-wide civil revolutions which will pass laws that ban medicines, mostly psychiatric drugs, abolish the professions of doctors, psychologists, and psychiatrists, in favor of in-depth diagnosis. It will be based on this lifetime and previous life, with the assistance of healers, mediums, and advanced alien technologies and frequency devices, without the intervention of medical staff.

Chapter 3:
The Aquarius Age

Age-rays: began since the year 1638.

The beginning of Age: from the year 2106.

The end of the Aquarius Age: with the entry of the Capricorn Age from the year 4212.

Aquarius Age's Circle 7 - Cyclicality 5: an age of correction, inventions and spirituality along with (5) love, unity, destruction of the old, rebuilding of the new order, with justice.

The Age-rays are always begun 468 years before the coming of the next age.

Calculation: **year 1638** = 2106 - 468. Sum digits of year 1638 = 1 + 6 + 3 + 8 = 18. Sum digits of 18 = 8 + 1 = 9.

Each Age lasts 2106 years and will end in the year 4212 = 2106 + 2106 = 4212. Sum digits of year 4212 = 4+2+1+2 = 9.

The sum of the Age digits or Age-rays is always 9 = completion and preparation for the new.

The Aquarius sign belongs to the planet Uranus (from the air signs and is symbolized by its waves.) ♒
This Aquarius Age comes to correct and to do justice with all that is distorted and corrupted. It's an Age of unity, discoveries, communication, and spiritualism, without governments but local communities, in which the power returns back to the masses, the citizens.

The properties of the Aquarius Age:

 Positive properties:

discovering the truth, doing fast justice, protecting freedom, uniting the citizens, by bringing the power back to them. The symbol of the Aquarius is air; therefore, inventions will be made from, air, gas, pressure, aviation, renewable energy, drones, and Tesla's wireless electricity and other devices, advanced scientific inventions based on alien's technologies.

Negative properties:

stubbornness, rebelliousness, impatience, innocence, and mental imbalance (mental = soul = air).

Signs of the Aquarius Age:

the Age-rays have been illuminated since the year 1638 AD, in which the scientist Galileo Galilei discovered that the Earth and nine planets circulate around the sun.

Over the next 90 years,
from the year 2016 to 2106:

technology will be accelerated; the power will return to the citizens which will bring justice and
a new world, many communities with female leadership will be established and human frequencies will undergo refinement.

"The wind and matter are waves
(as the sign of the Aquarius)
and the difference between them
is expressed in the intensity
of the frequency."

Human freedom and free faith
Replacing religions
There are no religions in the universe, but free faith

👍 **The Aquarius Age will fix the destruction of the Age of the Pisces:**

the Aquarius Age belongs to the air signs and is known for being spiritual. In the Aquarius Age, material religions will be replaced by free faith without matter, an age that will deal with spirituality, mysticism, channeling and the activation of the ten senses through intuition to telepathic communication. Everyone will integrate spirituality, receive messages, create spiritual art (mandalas), practice meditation and holistic healing methods, and more.

The symbol of the Age of the Pisces - a controlling and solitary man.

The symbol of the Aquarius Age - a woman, communities, and compassion.

In the Aquarius Age, Jesus will return in the image of many women who will bring knowledge, insights, and gospel to humanity.

There are no religions in the universe, but free faith.

Until about 100 years ago, dealing with spirituality was forbidden. In preparation for the coming Aquarius Age in the year 2106, *The Creation* brings to Earth new frequencies full of compassion, love, community involvement, unity, the discovery of truth, justice for all, respect and compassion for all living, towards world peace, which will start by men and continue by women.

The Aquarius is the sign of truth and justice; therefore, religious and spiritual methods of study will be released and exposed, knowledge that have been kept secret have begun to spread and were distributed over the past 1000's of years.

Religions are against human freedom and are administered out of material, therefore, religions, rituals, houses of worship, books of religion and religious occupations will be abolished in favor of free faith without matter.

An Age of convergence and love for others, to animals, nature, and the environment.

The Aquarius Age is an age of spirituality and mysticism, spiritual treatments and studies, understanding *The Creation,* predicting the future based on experience, professions of spiritual counseling, conversations with spirits and preparation for death, and discussions regarding it.

The barriers between religions will gradually be removed and consolidated.

Women will march to free faith and world-wide communities:

"There are no religions in the universe, but faith"

The material will never be holy - except for the soul, spirit.

Religion revolves around the matter and is contrary to human freedom. Religion is not spirituality.

In the approaching Aquarius Age, there will be free faith without matter.

As the level of education increases, religion will decline.

In the Age of the Pisces, man ruled through matter and religion. In the Aquarius Age, the woman will treat others with love without control or matter, with free faith without religion.

The Creation / God does not require a man to serve them, which is considered ancient pagan idolatry. The sacred is not in the material, stones, tombstones, religious books, prayer halls, ceremonies or religious clothing, all of which is associated with matter.

The power is in the hidden, in the personal faith, which is why humanity in the entire universe will never be able to discover details or the source of *The Creation* / God, for it is the mystery that drives all universe.

The Age of the Pisces began with the birth of Joshua / Jesus (year **0**):

a Jewish man who was ahead of his time by an age and brought the gospel to mankind, such as the abolition of religions and idolatry, God is love, and freedom for all. In the Age of the Pisces, the male ego was dominant, so religions did not exist in peace, but spread hatred through control, religious coercion, and even the extinction of the other, up until these days.

In order to cancel the religions, man will lead to religious radicalization. **"The beginning of each creation - requires chaos first"**.

In order to cancel the religions, chaos must be created, with extreme religious coercion. Therefore, the radical religious strength of all religions is expected to rise, especially in the case of race hatred, radical Islam against Judaism and Christianity, by violence against innocent civilians, prayer temples, terrorist acts, up to the annihilation of all religions.

In the Aquarius Age, Jesus will return as many women who will replace religions with free faith, compassion, tolerance, unity, and bring change to move humanity forward.

Cancellation of competitions

The sports, beauty, and music competitions will no longer exist, with the help of world-wide citizen revolutions. Awards and losses cause separation, the preference of one over the other, so it is not right to award prizes but to give a certificate of participation, if desired. You are all guests for a moment, please enjoy your journey.

In beauty and poetry competitions: is it important to find out who has a better look or voice? How does this promote humanity in any way? Every person is special, beauty and sound are based on personal taste, what is beautiful and pleasant to one is perhaps less beautiful and pleasant to another.

In sports competitions: swimming, running, tennis, soccer, basketball, etc... Is it really important to know which of the players has better physical ability? How do sports promote humanity? Or do they only magnify the ego and enrich individuals?

In mind competitions: chess, Sudoku, quizzes, etc.... Is it important to find out who has better mental abilities and memory? How does this promote humanity in any way? Or do they just glorify the ego of each participant?

Nobel Prizes: should be disqualified from existing because it's corrupted, since award winners are selected on the personal opinion of a team of "judges", individual opinion is not the general opinion. In the coming of the Aquarius Age, all of that will not take place. Most of the world's scientists will cooperate to advance humanity and not to win the Nobel prizes, they will all share and will be as pioneers.

Every competition is invalid because it creates discrimination and places one person above the other. A single prize does not promote humanity - but rather a collective action, which influences, and contributes to all.

In the Aquarius Age, most of the armies will be reduced until they are eliminated and military power will be replaced by friendly robots and cooperative digital machines, some of them human-like.

The Aquarius: the air sign
An age of inventions in air / gas movement

👍 **The Aquarius Age will fix the destruction of the Age of the Pisces:**

the sign of the Pisces is water; therefore, the technologies and innovations are related to water, creating energy using water pressure, pumping and burning fuel and oil. Additional ones were created, such as hydraulics, ships, submarines, dams, pools, Jacuzzi, sauna, hydroponic (water) therapies and more.

The sign of the Aquarius is air, it controls the movement of air / gas. Since the year 1638, from the beginning of the Aquarius Age-rays until today, the use of gas and air has intensified with a flying hot-air balloon, a fan, an air conditioner, hydraulic crane, wind turbines at sea and land, radio waves, satellites, high-speed aircraft, cell phones, laser, power waves, microwave waves, sound waves, light waves, smell waves, and nanotechnology.

Towards the beginning of the Aquarius Age in the year 2106, the use of electricity will be replaced from coal combustion, which produces carbon dioxide that traps heat in the atmosphere, to the use of non-polluting green energy. Only natural resources will be used to create energy - wind power, solar heat, magnets, frequencies, and more.

Extensive air traffic, equipment and propulsion using pressure, gas and space: massive use of frequencies, waves and gases. This will include the transport of objects, products and people on magnetic strips, in the air or inside capsules which maintain constant internal pressure and fly people and objects at tremendous speeds to their destination by gas, magnet, and air pressure.

Air traffic: the Aquarius Age as the air sign, will lead to innovations and inventions use by gas, air pressure and natural and green energy, flying vehicles, spaceships and a variety of aircraft, such as drones for deliveries, surveillance and broadcasting, and more.

All vehicles including flying vehicles and spacecraft will be equipped with magnets, sensors and algorithmic software to prevent injuries, so accidents cannot occur. In order to prevent accidents between aircraft and birds, the aircraft will be equipped with advanced equipment by sound and frequency in order to divert the flight of the birds from the aircraft.

Towards the Aquarius Age, there will be visits of spaceships from distant planets, combined with sightings and sounds. Humanity will meet their **Creators** and new life forms which will provide humanity with huge amounts of knowledge about space flight applications, including knowledge regarding the annulment of gravity from matter.

Borders will be removed, air-transport will connect continents and countries, citizens will be allowed to travel, live and work world-wide without work permits or visas. Residences will be granted via barter; world-wide communities will be established for all citizens under the leadership of women.

Green energy: the production of green independent energy will be used through the movement of wind and water, the heat which is stored on surfaces, roofs and roads, and the heat of the sun.

On the way to telepathic communication: in the Zodiac, the complementary sign in front of the Aquarius is the Lion and has a positive characteristic: the age of rebellion and the media, which represents the freedom of expression. Therefore, towards and during the Aquarius Age, power will return to the masses, to the citizens through world-wide civil revolutions combined with unifying social media. There will no longer be single corrupted media, which lies and makes profit from false propaganda and do not respect freedom of speech. It's an age of open communication and self-expression without fear. Technology and media tools will become faster, on the way to telepathic communication.

The Creation will always introduce knowledge and implement the change gradually:

first via a telephone dial - from there to a landline phone - to a wireless phone - to a cellular phone - to a wireless earphone - transmissions through an electric current and frequencies transmitted through the body - to the electrodes in the skull, accessories and optional chips (these temporary additional tools are for those who can't reach telepathic ability naturally) in the body until the realization of the lofty goal of: telepathic communication, just like our **Creators** / the extraterrestrials.

All this is in order to narrow the gap between humanity on Earth and other lifeforms in the universe and to push humanity to the 5th dimension, where people will finally experience total freedom, without fear.

Extensive use of electronic technologies:
technological devices will be miniaturized for nanomaterials and be optionally worn outside the human body, like a watch or necklace, or implanted into the human bodies, animals, machines, tools, soil, water, air, plants, in order to help, track, diagnose, repair, heal, cure, upgrade and communicate telepathically. Miniature flying machines in the shape of animals and objects will be built mostly for agricultural use.

Artificial intelligence:

Positive property: the production of robots with human appearance and extensive performance capabilities.

Negative property: developed robots will lead to their independent artificial intelligence and thinking, which might lead to the creation of Android (a combination of human and robot) in the shape of a human being, to assist humanity and replace corrupted people. These robots are run by justice and logical principles.

Freedom and human privacy

With the arrival of the Aquarius Age-rays, since the year 1638, the power gradually returned to the citizens through civil revolutions and wars with chaos, such as:

- The French Revolution: which lasted 10 years and brought to an end the period of monarchy and classes in France.

- The American Civil War: which led to the abolition of slavery, the enactment of a constitution and equal rights for citizens.

- World War I led to World War II: during that period *The Creation* led to the dilution of the world's population in order to free old-fashioned souls and replace them with new souls full of insight, love, and innovation.

- The War in Vietnam: ended thanks to the civil pressure and demonstrations in the United States.

- The fall of the Berlin Wall: the wall was broken down by a "divine error" in the Russian media and the power of the demonstration of the German citizens.

Until the beginning of the Aquarius Age, civil revolutions are expected to bring the destruction of governments, regimes, and monarchies, as it happened with the emperors of China and Japan, Hitler in Germany, Mussolini in Italy, Ceausescu in Romania, Saddam Hussein in Iraq, Mubarak in Egypt, etc.

Governments fear from the power of the masses and out of fear of their citizens, they created "internal security" to prevent citizen revolutions, by creating rules which harm human freedom.

The Earth's frequencies are becoming gentler, will affect all humanity, and will return the power to the citizens.

Since the year 1900, the signs of the Aquarius Age began to appear: the establishment of the United Nations, the use of politics to prevent wars and peacemaking, a significant improvement in human rights, laws for the protection of nature and animals, abolition of slavery and child labor, the establishment of a minimum age for marriage, The Industrial Revolution (machines which help humanity), environmental protection laws - animals and nature, rehabilitation of natural reservoirs, the release of animals from zoos and circuses and their return to nature, volunteering and the establishment of community associations.

World peace and world-wide communities.

Unity and human freedom
World peace and world-wide communities

The Aquarius Age will fix the destruction of the Age of the Pisces:

inequality and the division among citizens, classes, species and upper-class members will be eliminated. Borders between countries and the need for work visas will be removed. Governments, regimes, corrupted wealthy people will collapse. The purchase of properties will transition into public housing under a world-wide free living. People will become humble and less materialistic.

Until the entry of the Aquarius Age in the year 2106, the power will gradually return to citizens who will bring justice and order through civil revolutions combined with social media networks, trade, and unity. Women will lead and establish world-wide communities under world peace.

The borders are opening

The world-wide goal to open the borders and unite humanity, will force people to wander and work everywhere, since every new creation requires chaos first: **"The beginning of each creation - requires chaos first".**

Therefore, skilled and professional manpower crossings are expected. With the transitions between countries through chaos, civilians will flee and immigrate as refugees to various countries. Dictators, monarchies, and governments will gradually collapse and the boundaries will be removed, thanks to the power of the citizens.

World Union

Borders between countries will disappear and with them the isolation of Earth in the universe. Humanity will become 'world-wide villages', yet refugees from foreign countries who will be violent towards the local citizens will be punished heavily, even with death penalty, and mostly thrown out by the communities. Everything that happens is not accidental but guidance from *The Creation* in order to unite humanity.

The Creation creates chaos which causes citizens to flee their country, to inspire other countries, to take an interest in the processes that take place outside their own country, **because once the 'problem' comes to your place – only then you become aware and involved.** Everything that happens in one country will affect all the inhabitants on Earth. Aquarius Age is about responsibility, caring, collective unity, and all for the sake of others.

The Creation has given humans the innovations of media and communications through the Internet. The signs of the union of humanity have accelerated since the year of 1998, with the establishment of Google and social media networks which provide knowledge which empowers the masses with world unification, self-expression, the need to remove and correct the corruptions. In the future, all the knowledge of the people will be gathered in knowledge banks for the benefit of the next generations. This will get rid of the corrupt and create a comfortable community life for everyone by sharing the wealth with all.

Reduction of consumption

The Age of Pisces has brought to the population of developed countries abundance, luxury life, brands, and an increased consumption culture. The transition between the end of that Age and the beginning of the Aquarius Age will be accompanied by extremism and chaos: "The beginning of each creation - requires chaos first".

And so, towards the beginning of the Aquarius Age until the year 2106, the world-wide consumption grows to enormous proportions, less domestic production, more imports, and with it a world-wide waste of plastic, nylon, cans, metals, technological equipment, medical equipment, etc...

Poor countries will become the wastebasket of rich countries, for example: piles of clothes are buried in African soil and piles of recycled computer accessories are sent to China. This process will not be allowed towards the year 2106 and each country will be obliged to recycle its own garbage.

Earth's frequencies will continue to refine and affect all life on Earth, and humanity will have the insights to live in moderation and modesty, through recycling and consumables, independent production and community acquisition.

In the Aquarius Age, the number of consumer products of each person will be significantly reduced to few items of clothing made by recycled, natural cotton with bright colors. Products of plastic and polycarbonate will be replaced with natural and recycled materials and consumables, such as ceramic / glassware, wood, etc... Consumer goods and household waste will be recycled. Medical equipment, dishes, utensils, and personal shower will use air pressure and vacuum, instead of cleaning them with water, because we are departing from the Pisces Age's water.

Restrict advertising

The Aquarius Age has come to correct and clean the environment from outdoor advertising, because the public space belongs to the general public!

Public approval should be sought for all outdoor advertising and should not be a distraction, in order to preserve human freedom. It is prohibited to pollute the public environment, water, air, and soil.   Hence, advertising at written publication media, digital signage, and even voice advertising during telephone waiting times - will all be prohibited!

Any advertising media that does not allow a person to shut down, silence, or conceal it and belongs to the public space, will be prohibited by law.

Residence

In the Age of the Pisces, humans emerged from the family tribe to live in a small family unit (Divide and Conquer), albeit with privacy and independence but with a touch of loneliness. That Age is characterized by the love of money and property, so the purchase of land and property was common, which caused a person to become enslaved to taxes, debts, and materials, in the long term instead of enjoying the money accumulated here and now. In the approaching Aquarius Age, humanity will return to living in world-wide communities and tribes. It will be a life without material, multiple movements, and property acquisition, but with a free world-wide living.

The accumulation of matter will gradually disappear. Residential buildings will be built by communities as public housing for the entire population with a cost-free lease and without purchase (if you cause damage, you will repair it for the satisfaction of the community). It will be possible to lease the residential buildings long-term, but not to purchase them, and everyone will be able to live where they wish. This will gain momentum towards the establishment of world-wide communities with female leadership.

In this way, humanity will move with no commitment to the material and will make living be like free dynamic tourism, in which the borders will be removed and people will be able to live wherever they want without visas.

In the coming of the Aquarius Age, humanity will emerge from loneliness, and communities will flourish and connect people through the internet and social media networks, sharing, volunteering, helping the community and environment to the benefits of others.

The old method of living in a man-woman-child cell will be transformed into a family unit which requires higher education, license to become parents. In the future the family unit will mainly be made of a single gender, woman or man, or an Android (half human and half robot), or living in a group, a tribe, or a community. This will build an upgraded population with higher education, with fewer chances of crime.

Everything is designed by *The Creation* to narrow the gaps between humanity on Earth and other forms of life in the universe, in order to meet with our *Creators,* the extraterrestrials, and other living forms from distant planets, which is expected to take place as we are entering the Aquarius Age.

The Age of the Woman
A Feminist leadership for World Peace

👍 **The Aquarius Age will fix the destruction of the Age of the Pisces:**

we are now departing from the Age of the Pisces, during which the man defined borders, ruled, created governmental and business corruption and caused wars. In the Aquarius Age, the woman will rise, love and compassion will lead, the truth will be revealed and justice will be done with each person.

The borders will be removed, on the way to world-wide communities for all citizens under a feminist world peace leadership. In the Aquarius Age, Jesus will return to Earth in the form of many women who will bring news gospel to humanity, with high intuition, extensive preoccupation with spirituality, and the exchange of religions to free faith.

Therefore, *The Creation* "abuses" women for thousands of years in order to awaken and empower them:

the signs of the Aquarius Age: women have struggled to obtain the right to vote since the end of the 18th century, and only did so approximately 100 years ago (around 1920). Also, from the end of the 18th century, in parallel with their work at home, women left the house to work in shops, workshops and industry, munitions factories during World Wars and since then women's organizations have been established. Women will replace men in world leadership under world peace.

Because of a lack of justice and equal rights, nowadays women are more independent, motivated, and struggle for their rights, they do not give in to violence, and choose not to marry and file for divorce, and choose in advance to become a single parent.

In order to exercise their freedom of choice, women will not want to have children, and therefore the population is supposed to be reduced gradually and naturally, within 200 years, as we are entering the Aquarius Age. This is humanity's destiny, the divine natural plan of God / *The Creation.*

Unfortunately, there are wealthy wicked people, who are familiar with this plan of *The Creation* **and might want to take shortcuts to achieve the same amount of population reduction within a shorter period of time, by creating their own evil plan, using a man-made global pandemic.**

Over the years, these wealthy wicked people bought the world's mainstream media, in order to create a false reality for their own benefits, with the use of lies, propaganda, and brainwash. Their evil plan was also to promote toxic vaccinations, in order to reduce the same amount of population within 10 years, instead of 200 years. This is considered a global genocide!

The final amount of the population reduction will always stay the same, because you cannot change destiny, but only exercise your freedom of choice to choose a different timeline, either expedite or delay it.

The complementary sign in the Zodiac, opposite to the Aquarius sign is Leo and has a positive characteristic, communication and media. Women will be able to lead the media, civil revolutions, gain equality and fill senior positions of judges, directors and other executive positions.

The Leo Age has a negative characteristic, which is it's known for its pride and ego, its desire to rule, to lead, and to impose an opinion. Therefore, in the Aquarius Age, there are struggles between men who want to control and women who want freedom to lead their own lives and others, which be achieved only through chaos.

The corrupt powerful old world will collapse, along with sects and terrorist organizations, the collapse of all religions and their replacement by free faith, regimes and governments, dictatorships, corrupt public figures, banks, insurance companies and financial institutions, Scientology, cults, racial, and anti-Semitic groups. All that will happen through world-wide civil revolutions.

Exposing the truth and doing justice
All human actions return to him during his lifetime

👍 **The Aquarius Age will fix the destruction of the Age of the Pisces:**

this new age will dismantle the old by doing justice through citizen revolutions, exposing the truth and discovering irregularities and corruption within governments, an election fraud with cyberattacks, regimes, public figures, institutions, organizations, and businessmen. All the corrupt will collapse and disappear.

It will be accepted that there is no need for multiple governments, since all citizens are seeking the same living conditions and then governments will vanish in favor of the establishment of world-wide communities.

World-wide Communities

To be established for the benefit of all citizens, every citizen will receive an ID number as 'Citizen of Earth'. Women will lead through world-wide revolutions, world-wide peace, and the creation of communities on a variety of issues in order to do justice and create new laws.

Governments, the European Union, the UN, and other powerful world organizations will be abolished as a result of high corruptions, election frauds, while citizens will be able to express their opinion and influence quickly.

Justice will be done with each person here and now: "All the acts of a person return to him during his lifetime".

Human freedom

Freedom is the symbol of the Aquarius Age, freedom of expression and choice. Advanced technologies and media will contribute to the discovery and exposure of the truth by world-wide civil revolutions, to restore order and justice.

"The beginning of each creation - requires chaos first",
therefore, *The Creation* will abuse civilians, by raising to power corrupt elected officials and hoax pandemics which will prevent human freedom, in order for the civilians to rise up, rebel, and return their power to themselves.

The frequencies of the Earth are refining with more compassion, unity, and caring.

In fear of losing power, governments, corporations, and institutions will follow, tap, and spy on citizens with advanced technologies such as chips, surveillance cameras and robots, using "defense, prevention, and homeland security" as excuses. These actions will be prohibited by law during the Aquarius Age, in order to protect human privacy and freedom.

You can't develop independent people and logical thinking, without taking away their own freedom at the beginning. Each creation requires chaos first. *The Creation* takes away, in order for people to reach for and complete the missing.

Power returns to the masses

Democratic-capitalist governance methods will be forced to change in favor of collective civil welfare. Regimes and dictators, monarchies and governments will collapse. In this age, the order will be made only by the masses rather than a powerful single power. World-wide civil revolutions will eliminate poverty, bring about just and equal legislation and the dismantling of wealth from the rich and its distribution to all citizens of the world.

Cancellation of individual representative

In the Aquarius Age, the individual representative will cease, such as the cancellation of the position of prime minister, heads of organizations and chairman, in which the communities and people's councils will express the will of the citizens in order for people to express themselves without mediators. The voice of the individual will be heard and will backed by the group, because the power is in the groups, communities, and masses.

Civil revolutions

Civil revolutions influence the masses to change their life quality! The power is in the hands of the masses and not in corrupted people or governments. The world's wealth will be divided equally among all people. It is impossible to harass, abuse and intimidate populations non-stop. People were not born to pay taxes all their lives, as this is not a living, but slavery. People will no longer be products of the corporative governments. Successful civil revolutions require collaboration with security forces, such as the police and army. Remember, at the beginning these security forces will go against the citizens, as they do what they were paid for, until they will realize that they are citizens themselves first and the benefits of the revolutions will benefit them and their families for sake of the next generations. You must approach the security forces with compassion, tolerance, knowledge, and mind and not violence, which will lead to violence. This is what the new Aquarius Age is all about. There will always be victims who will pay with their lives in order to awaken the others, it is impossible for the security forces to shoot and kill the whole entire population!

Remember - you cannot die, you are an infinite spirit, which will return and receive a new life in another body, if you want to, while you choose without an ego. **When you understand this, the priorities will change.**

Governments fear from the power of their citizens, with the thought that the destruction will rise from within, rather than from outside wars, so internal security forces were invented. **Governments plan and execute terrorist attacks world-wide** in order to maintain wars, preserve fear and the brainwash of citizens, control and navigate the countries from afar, in order to receive public support for non-democratic actions.

Do not believe in the mainstream media which serves the needs of governments and are being paid off by them. Instead, investigate and reach for information from the citizens, through the social media.

THE AQUARIUS AGE   125

During the Aquarius Age, there won't be armies, but world-peace and police will be replaced by civilian protection.

Collecting weapons from civilians

In countries where the purchase of weapons is permitted (such as the United States, Arab states, etc...), the sale will be limited it will be completely forbidden, following many cases of innocent civilians being killed, especially while we are entering world peace, in which one will protect the other.

Laws will be established in the United States which will require the collection of weapons and the restoration of order. The real war is against the arms companies and their lobbyists in Congress, who are working out of greed of money, so exposing the truth will cause them to collapse.

Laws will be enacted in the world to reduce the quantities of civilian weapons and additional laws which would prohibit civilians from acquiring and owning weapons. Despite the opponents, the process will gradually materialize as humanity enters the Aquarius Age. This will lead to world-wide chaos, especially in Arab countries, and in the US in particular.

Weapons will be collected by the security forces and army with the help of soldiers, robots, and tanks. Under the influence of the refining of Earth frequencies, most civilians will return their weapons without resistance and will receive a refund from the arms companies.

The opponents will be fortified and risk their lives, yet the weapons will be taken away by the army. This will take place world-wide.

In the Aquarius Age, which has already begun, "all actions return to the person during his lifetime" and therefore, any action will cause the karma to return, albeit positive or negative. **All the corrupt will collapse and disappear using the new weapon of the citizens, which is revealing the truth.**

English the international language
The native language of all citizens

👍 The Aquarius Age will fix the destruction of the Age of the Pisces:

spreading the English language worldwide began with the expansion and conquest of the British Empire. *The Creation* pushed the British Empire to expand around the world, with the aim of spreading the English language and culture, yet citizens tend to fight for reasons such as ego, the need to "be unique", ignorance, and not seeing the potential future benefit.

Countries where citizens **have not fought** against the British occupation, are now experiencing a revival, progress, and better quality of life under British rule, such as Ireland, Australia, New Zealand, and South Africa. Yet, when the British empire will collapse, then Britain and these countries will suffer from chaos and the loss of power, at the beginning.

On the other hand, there are countries which were conquered by the British Empire but fought for their independence and in retrospect, they lost language, progress, and culture, such as India, the United States, Canada, Hong Kong, Sri Lanka, Burma, Jordan, Iraq, Kuwait, Oman, Yemen, Qatar, Egypt, Israel, Sudan, Nigeria, Kenya, and Uganda.

Think for a moment, what kind of rejuvenation and quality of life improvement would have taken place in these countries.

Over 90 years, from the year 2016 until the beginning of the Aquarius Age in the year 2106, the English language will gradually become the mother tongue of the world.

Some will try to preserve the source language but it will fade over time. Communication technologies will be accelerated to telepathy. Following the change of language there will be chaos between the old world and the new world.

Even today, in order to communicate with the rest of the world, the English language is used in tourism, stock exchange, business, internet, passports, high-tech, science, medicine, politics, education, online games, social media, etc.

For anyone who wants progress and quality, it is best for him to connect with the positive culture, language, patience, refinement, and courtesy of the British nation, yet avoid the negative aspects of the British culture.

Barter
Switch from virtual currency to barter

👍 **The Aquarius Age will fix the destruction of the Age of the Pisces:**

we are now departing from the Age of the Pisces, in which man dominated the material, money, banks, loans, debt, stock exchanges, investment houses, insurance companies, tobacco, arms companies, pharmaceuticals, and other corrupt corporations which have caused citizens to enslave themselves for hundreds of years.

As we enter the Aquarius Age, all these institutions will collapse and disappear thanks to the world-wide civil revolutions which will reveal the truth, do justice, and create a new world which will benefit the public and makes Earth a better place to live. The wealth does not belong to individuals but to all public.

In the Aquarius Age, the money bills and coins will be replaced from tangible currency to virtual ones. The currencies and bills, coins, checks, and credit cards will first be replaced by a virtual bank such as PayPal, banking transactions via electronic screens / fingerprint / voice & DNA recognition and personal code, and from there to trade without a material currency, but for barters, exchanging knowledge, goods, technology, and more.

The need for unity and collective exchange will increase with transnational volunteerism. The employment of citizens will be replaced from work as employees to work as self-employed. In that way everyone will become independent, trade knowledge within communities. They will share spaces for offices, work from home / nature / public places or parks, with a high need to combine animals and plants in a workspace or in the living environment.

At the beginning of the Aquarius Age, the transition from the use of material money to the use of virtual exchange will also bring cyberattacks and hackers into the fight. This will cause damages, thefts, and disruptions on behalf of private people or public organizations.

The environment
Cleaning and maintaining nature

The Aquarius Age will fix the destruction of the Age of the Pisces:

in the Aquarius Age, there is a supreme principle to repair, cure, and restore from the destruction of the Age of the Pisces, as well as protecting all nature around, such as humans, animals and natural resources at sea, land, and air. The Earth reminds humanity that for billions of years of its existence it cannot be destroyed, yet only the human life can.

"All humans' actions return to them as karma":
the moment a person destroys the elements of nature, then the forces of nature will strike back, bring natural disasters on humanity, and the climate will become extreme.

Humans will try to control climate conditions, but will not succeed.

Citizens will have to eliminate governments in order to save human lives and achieve freedom. World-wide laws will be enacted to reduce pollution and preserve nature reserves.

Destruction of natural resources will never affect the survival of Earth, but only the survival of mankind and all the living inhabiting it temporarily.

Human-kind only understands through destruction and chaos; therefore, *The Creation* will bring natural disasters that will continue into the Aquarius Age:

• **The drought in Africa,** emerges from extreme industrialization of major countries which are burning huge quantities of coal, that releases carbon dioxide, and gets trapped in the atmosphere. **Everything that happens in one area on Earth, affects the rest of the planet; therefore, citizens worldwide will understand they must cooperate and help each other for the benefit of all.**

• **Many natural disasters will return as a Karma to damage in the heavy polluting continents:**

▪ Asia - China: China's mainland is expected to suffer from sinkholes, tsunamis, and sea water will gradually cover the entire continent, **until it will completely sink under the sea towards the Aquarius Age.**

▪ The United States will suffer from warming, earthquakes, swallowing pits, extreme heat and hurricanes. Coastal areas will be flooded. The United States will rebuild itself as a new republic, with new advanced and free technologies which will benefit the environment and human quality of life, that will set an example for the rest of the world.

Cleaning the natural reservoirs

While we are entering the Aquarius Age, Earth's frequencies are constantly affecting humanity, animals and natural reservoirs, and new insights enter. Governments will "abuse" their citizens in order to cause them to rebel, in order for citizens to bring justice by eliminating governments, which are the main problem. Any institute which will not respect the human freedom, will collapse and disappear, thanks to the power of the masses.

The massive cleaning effort will include:

• **Conservation of the environment:** cleaning of natural resources, beaches, lakes, seas, forests and cities, as well as the closing of refineries and polluting factories.

• **Cleaning of the air:** using huge blowers and filters. Climate engineering and chemical spraying will be strictly prohibited.

• **Cleaning of the lands:** by frequency and transmission devices, air pressure, gases, and more. Hydroponic agricultural cultivation without soil will also be leveraged.

• **Cleaning of the water reservoirs:** groundwater, rivers, lakes, oceans, lands, and seawaters will undergo purifications.

• **Cleaning of the Sewage:** filtration and cleaning will be carried out in desalination plants and will return to faucets as drinking water, daily use water, and irrigation water.

• **Waste recycling:** for the production of clean energy will include usage of natural resources, mainly air / gas and solar heat, for natural production of energy.

Recycling

Over the next 90 years, between the years 2016 - 2106 as humanity enters the Aquarius Age, the landfill will gradually disappear, and will be recycled in domestic and friendly enterprises and technologies in garbage recycling facilities.

Garbage dumps will be banned and the garbage will be converted into clean energy which will return as gas, soil, and reusable materials.

Recycling, refurbishing and manufacturing of products from recycled agricultural growth and materials will take place.

Everything is natural and cyclical - that is why humanity will adjust itself to it.

Releasing the animals

Animals from zoos, circuses, and cages will return to nature. At first, they'll return to natural reserves under human supervision, with equipment for surveillance and technological protection, and later on to plots of land and islands free from man (such as the Galapagos Islands). Laws will be enacted to protect all-natural reservoirs and animals.

Animal abuse and hunting will be prohibited. Any human who takes the lives of animals, will pay with their own lives, except for the eating of fish (not dolphins, whales, or seafood), because we are departing from the Pisces Age.

Eating animals will be banned, except for fish. The transition to vegetarianism and veganism will become common and scientifically proven as healthy, as opposed to eating meat which is a major cause of diseases. **This is because the man was created by mixing DNA between a male gorilla eating plants and a female alien.**

Communication with all the surrounding living

Following the transformation of frequencies on Earth, an energetic connection between humans and animals and the entire nature is expected, which will heal and help each other and all the living forms in and out planet Earth. Humans will develop communication and mutual contact between animals, plants, trees, earth, light, air, and aliens, all of which contain frequencies. The main frequency of compassion will affect all surroundings.

Nature has always spoken, but humans never listened, and now humans are getting the insights that nature around them is not inanimate, yet is alive and communicates.

It is not possible to kill, destroy or eliminate anything on Earth or in the entire universe, but only to change the states of matter, because during life spirit becomes matter and during death returns to back to spirit.

Every tree or plant that will be cut, will grow again.

Any reservoir of land or sea that has been contaminated - will be naturally cleaned again.

Every man who dies, his soul returns back to spirit and can reincarnate again.

The sea water evaporates and returns as rain, which flows into rivers, lakes, oceans and sea, and so forth.

Everything cycles forever! You can't destroy anything.

Transitions always cycle between three transform states: solid - liquid - gas.

All matter around a soul, which changes states:

the soul (spirit, gas) enters the body of matter (solid contains fluids) and breathes life into it (soul). At some point, it ends its journey, exits the material and returns to its original state (as spirit, gas). If you wish, the spirit will breathe again (soul) into a material body (solid) and return again.

Eating healthy, and adjusted
Vegetarianism, veganism and independently grown crops

The Aquarius Age will fix the destruction of the Age of the Pisces:

in the Aquarius Age, power is restored to the citizens, who will march humanity towards vegetarianism and nature, compassion for animals, organic & biological pest control:

- Citizens will live in modesty with less consumption without waste.
- Independently grown crops will be purchased from each other and local growers.
- Fresh raw materials from nature will be used.
- Dishes will be prepared fresh on a daily basis and from leftovers.
- Cooking and baking tools 'as the old-fashioned way' will be used, as they are natural and healthy.

The Aquarius Age will bring compassion and universal love, the citizens will understand the importance of nature, animals, and empathy. Killings and slaughtering will be banned.

The Creation will cause chaos (in order to create changes) by producing diseases and viruses in animals, in order to prevent humans from consuming them. Only when human health is at risk, then humans avoid consuming animals.

Humanity will understand that we were originally created from the gorillas as plant eaters and that meat eating stemmed from the default of ancient man to survive in times of droughts. Therefore, from that evolved a species of man with fangs. Eating meat is not suitable for humans and in the long term is harmful and causes physical diseases.

The medicine of the future will be based on personal DNA and will prove that unlike predators, the human body was created from a mixing between a male gorilla and female alien which both cannot digest meat without producing long-term illnesses.

Custom food according to a personal DNA

Future medicine will also prove that **consuming foods that are not personalized to each person's DNA level - can lead to health problems,** such as: allergies, diabetes, colitis, cancer, osteoporosis, Alzheimer's, obesity, Crohn and other diseases.

Each person, animal and plant will have a personal DNA test, and based on their frequencies results, a detailed personal report defining the types of compatible food, similar to a personal menu, will be provided.

The consumption of dairy products will be discouraged.

Just as animals do not feed on a woman's breast milk, so humans must not consume milk from animals because it disrupts human's DNA.

Humans are born different; every person has a different diet adapted to his individual DNA coils level.

Do not mix with animal DNA. Eat fruits, vegetables; herbs, legumes, and whole grains.

The damages of sugar and wheat

Since the 1950s, with the population growth, the production of food became industrialized, made of low quality and non-nutritious products. The food was engineered and the grains were sprayed with chemicals, in order to supply large quantities of produce, regardless of its low quality and non-nutritiousness. They did not consider the future health damage results to the consumer public.

Now we can examine the devastating health consequences such as obesity, diabetes, osteoporosis, cancer, and other diseases.

If the modern medicine is so advanced - then why do the number of patients and hospitals grow each year?

Technology and science have led to an increase in life expectancy on the one hand, and on the other, to an increase in the number of hospitals, diseases, patients and medicines. This is an illogical paradox, because the health organizations and governments create diseases, which are patented, in order to dilute the population, create dependence and slavery, consumers of medicine, doctors, and other professions, surgeries, medical treatments. All of this translates into tons of money each year.

It is not the vaccinations which prevent disease, but a dramatic rise in world-wide hygiene. All vaccinations weaken the immune system. Because of that, towards the Aquarius Age, all vaccinations will be banned, after worldwide chaos from the pharmaceutical organization, that will try to force vaccination on the population. However, the masses will unite and uprise, by creating a new free world.

Every disease stems from the soul, so the future medicine will combine spiritual healers, psychics, and advance and natural technology, based on frequencies and DNA repair.

The Age-rays of the Aquarius have already begun to correct the community health by bringing awareness to humanity regarding the importance of a healthy life-style.

Under the influence of the purchasing power of citizens, laws will be enacted on Earth, such as the:

- Prohibition of adding sugar. Substitutes and artificial sweeteners in food and drink products will also be prohibited in general, but only natural sweeteners with minimal consumption will be allowed.

- Prohibition of selling junk food or any food without nutrients.

- Prohibition of using engineered wheat, legumes and grains and their consumption, with high-fiber.

Following a world-wide movement of women and parents, healthy eating laws will be passed for children, students, patients, the elderly, and consumers.

Grants will be awarded for local and independent agricultural cultivation.

As we are approaching the year 2106, the beginning of the Aquarius Age, we will see a healthy movement on cooking and baking, mainly on social media, such as vegetarianism and veganism, the preparation of healthy drinks, natural and organic ingredients, self-cultivation from fruits, vegetables, legumes, sprouting, and more.

The Aquarius Age belongs to the sign of air; therefore, we will see an extension in private agricultural crops and in greenhouses or in warehouses on air, without land.

Nutrition affects human health. Companies and food companies which produce junk food will be prohibited. Nutritionists in educational, health, and public institutions will be forced to provide a varied and healthy menu, which will be chosen by consumers. Publication and financing of junk food in public institutions will be prohibited.

Prohibition of eating animals and drinking milk from them

Only a pregnant cow gives milk, so it is constantly fertilized by hormones that reach the milk products and cause allergies and diseases. It's unhealthy to mix foods and drinks which contain different DNA between different species.

Plant pest control

Following the mass transit to organic food, farmers will be forced to switch to organic / plant-free pesticides and biological pest control, and engineered bugs for crop protection. Dramatic increase in home-grown, communal and available agriculture is expected in every available plot of land, even on roofs, balconies, and public areas.

Control of population growth
Parental certification and a parenting license

👍 **The Aquarius Age will fix the destruction of the Age of the Pisces:**

today, the world's population is about **7.5** billion people, a huge amount on one planet which is supposed to provide protection, shelter, food, and drinking water for everyone. *The Creation* warns humanity from mass population growth, otherwise there will be a huge shortage of drinking water, food, housing, and human survival.

During the Aquarius Age, women will live mostly in female communities, some in which men will not be allowed to enter. Because of that, there is an increased movement today of males who change their gender to females, in order to build a foundation for future generations to be able to enter these female communities and take over female leadership roles, especially when the devil enjoys switching the genders of humans.

The Creation will provide insights to humans, in order to solve issues by means of laws:

'License to become a parent':

adults who have been trained and licensed mentally, economically, educationally, and socially will be able to have a license to become parents of their biological children or other people's, as is currently required for a driver's license, building permit, sales license, occupation license, and others.

Uncontrolled childbirth has an adverse effect on the progress of humanity. It is inconceivable that adults and teenagers will have children as they wish, as if they were purchasing objects, without qualifying them as parents through a license for parental competence before bringing children. Is it logical for parental competence to be tested nowadays after birth? It is absurd.

Parenting is the most difficult task of any future generations. Parents are responsible for educating their children. Schools do not educate, but only expand knowledge, which can be done independently using the Internet and social media.

This law will first be accepted with civil resistance which will become more acceptable over the years. Citizens who will violate the law and bring children without a license, their children will instead be placed among parents with license.

You did not come to Earth in order to bring children, this need comes from egoistic human survival. You are here to 'Create' which means to invent, in order to consistently move forwards *The Creation's* engine. And that's not by having lots of children!

Birth Control Law

Childbirth will be limited by control and fertility treatments for men and women, especially in countries with high population, all in order to reduce the population and prevent future wars of survival for food, drinking water, and living space.

Abortion is not murder, because the newborn's soul does not reside in the pregnant woman's body, but enters the fetus' body only when the first breath is taken during birth.

Natural dilution of the population

"The beginning of each creation - requires chaos first"

Therefore, towards the beginning of the Aquarius Age from the year 2106, natural disasters and disease outbreaks are expected to dilute the population by the actions of the mostly corrupted men, which have advanced technology to control the weather, using extreme climatic conditions, such as extreme heat and cold, freezing, massive rain and hail, sandstorms, sinkholes, typhoons, hurricanes, tsunamis, and floods. All of this, is the corrupted human taking shortcuts, playing God in order to dilute the population. Remember, everything you do, will come back to you, in this lifetime.

Africa and India

Today, the population of Africa is about 1.2 billion people, and the population of India is about 1.3 billion people.

The reasons for the failure of these places are:

- Lack of control over the birth rate which causes population growth.

- Opposition to progress and modernization.

- Lack of education, agriculture, and technology.

- An old-fashioned culture of male laziness, ego, and enslavement of women.

- Outdated religious practices, extreme class differences, and high corruption.

- Rising food prices due to massive purchases by developing countries.

- Other countries sponsoring civil wars and depleting the natural resources of these countries.

- Failed places such as Africa, India and others, must receive the help of other countries. These failed countries will be given assistance, knowledge, financial compensation, and supervision from the countries that damaged them. This is a karma closure.

The African continent is the next continent to rise and grow in the Aquarius Age, thanks to a world-wide female leadership and worldwide communities.

China

Today, over one billion Chinese citizens are under communist rule which does not allow freedom and equal rights. *The Creation* does not respect **the Chinese people who do not respect the code of life,** consume fetuses, dogs, kidnap children in mass, enslave each other, and are the most cowardly! It is easy to control Asians, because their DNA is mostly from aliens. Therefore, they have less emotions and they behave similar to robots, which are easy to control.

That is why **the Chinese people** are so disciplined, obedient, non-rebellious, and even help the tyrannical regime "maintain order." This communist regime employs a huge number of policemen, law and order people, and even spies. The Chinese regime is afraid from the power of its citizens who may rebel and overthrow the regime; therefore, the regime has established strict laws and does not allow the following: democracy with freedom, connection to world-wide social networks and world media channels.

Towards the Aquarius Age, this regime will collapse by powerful countries with the assistance of some brave Chinese people, just like other regimes, empires, governments and monarchies which will collapse and vanish. The power will return to the citizens, only through chaos.

China's mainland is expected to suffer from sinkholes, tsunamis, the collapse of dams, and sea water which will gradually cover the entire continent, until China will completely sink under the sea towards the Aquarius Age.

Mental Illness

The Aquarius Age is a spiritual age which will bring the spirituality to its peak. Frequencies that are refined into Earth will affect all humanity; therefore, using healers and psychics will become common.

Spirituality at its peak also has a negative aspect, which will manifest itself in various mental illnesses that will be treated by spiritual methods, advanced alien technologies, healers and psychics, who know how to treat the soul, which diseases originate from and complete a closure from previous lives.

Psychiatric medicines will be outlawed because it will be proven that these medicines cause damage and long-term addiction. The spirit cannot be treated with material, but only with spiritual roles, such as psychics and healers.

Psychologists and psychiatrists will be outlawed, only psychics and healers, combined with advanced alien technologies, will have the access and permission to treat patients.

People will be offered to prepare a Death Will, an option to die legally whenever they ask for.

Every person borrows a soul and chooses the date of the entry of his soul into the physical body which he inhabits, and the date of the exit of the soul from the human body.

It is permissible to commit suicide, to ask to die, as long as the choice was made freely, consciously and with clear mind, without any third-party which forced it to do so.

The universal law states that above all, no-one may dismiss the human freedom of choice, even God / *The Creation* can't do so, as they will always provide humans with a free will to choose.

You cannot die!
This is because you can't kill the spirit or soul, they are endless, death is a gift to open a new incarnation page.

Education and re-education
World-wide knowledge-sharing

👍 **The Aquarius Age will fix the destruction of the Age of the Pisces:**

Education

Since the 1960s, there has been a gradual change in education, protection and recognition of the rights of children, inexpensive education for all children and a constant change of the world-wide education system, thanks to the revolutions of the wonderful children with ADHD.

Towards the Aquarius Age, educational and institutional systems will be upgraded to small study groups, digital education methods, less theoretical and more practical. There will be virtual and holographic teachers and robots on campuses and community centers with an emphasis on independent creation and inventions, science and technology, art, music, the environment, and more. **Grades and assessments will be eliminated, as well as the concept of 'student' in favor of a new one called 'knowledger'.**

Educational institutions do not educate but enrich knowledge!

Each student will choose the topics of study in which he or she is interested and will be examined on them without receiving a grade, but a graduation certificate.

Classes will be eliminated and the knowledger will be classified according to the level of knowledge he has accumulated. Academic degrees will be cancelled. Study subjects that discuss historical events, such as history and religion, will be classified as general knowledge, because they do not contribute to the future of humanity.

As long as people continue hating one another, it is a sign that human beings have not learned anything from the mistakes of the past.

What have we learned from history lessons?

For example, during World War II, the United States dropped two atomic bombs on Japan's cities, Hiroshima and Nagasaki, causing extensive destruction and hundreds of thousands of deaths. However, countries have still succeeded in acquiring atomic bombs for deterrence and defense. During the Aquarius Age, **ALL** weapons will be dismantled, in favor of world peace.

Only advanced education and technology will connect humanity on Earth and other life forms in the universe.

New Age Children

Education on Earth is developing greatly thanks to the entry of the crystal and indigo children, who were born since 1945 onwards. These children have high spiritual frequencies and abilities, a burst of energy and necessary curiosity. They were labeled as ADHD's Children.

There is no accidentalness in the universe, but a divine plan for everything that happens!

These precious souls came to Earth to implement several goals:

Indigo children: are souls from distant planets, extraterrestrial geniuses with analytic thinking, they came to speed up the technology and reduce the gap between us and our *Creators*, the aliens, in order to meet and communicate with them telepathically.

Crystal children: are spiritual and refined children, curious, are protein consumers, with high frequencies and senses, almond eyes, and they usually require quiet and privacy. They came to raise humanity's level of compassion, morality, unity, and caring.

Indigo and crystal children are designed to create revolutions, in order to change the outdated rigid learning system by learning such as: small groups and online, advanced digital learning methods, learning outside the classroom and studying out at the nature and from the community. People, both children and adults, will learn without competition / evaluations or grades, which do not attest to the person's ability!

Educational institutions will adjust themselves to the needs of all who wish to learn. Nowadays, children and students must adjust themselves to the learning subjects of the education system, without free will to choose. This will end because only the people will create, develop, and choose the learning subjects.

The old world will collapse and disappear. These curious children are requesting: "Don't tell me, but show me."

The Creation **forbids drugging and poisoning** these children with ADHD, with psychiatric medicines which disrupt their wonderful frequencies. All in order to adapt them to the rest of the people, turn them into robots and create a quiet environment for teachers. These medicines take away from them their curiosity and their natural activeness.

They came to Earth with high levels of energy and frequencies to produce revolutions, to ask hard questions, and to repair the faulty systems from within.

The nature of the problem lies in the old school system and not in them!!

Psychiatric medicines are like illegal drugs! They disrupt the brain cells and cause future needs for eating disorders, hormonal problems and sleep, OCD, tics in the head and body, neurological problems, social disruption, lack of self-confidence, and more. These medicines will be outlawed, thanks to universal parental pressure.

Following pressure from the parents in the world, psychiatric medicines will become outlawed.

When there is a hole in the road (the old-fashioned education system), will you repair the hole or would you prefer to take a drug to create a virtual reality in which the hole has already been fixed?

Re-education of criminals / prisoners:
will be given the opportunity to correct their way in 're-education villages'. Prisoners who are released to the community and return to crime will be given the opportunity to improve themselves several times up, in order for them not to harm the society, but to be of benefit to the community. If a person will continue doing harm to others repeatedly, after the community invested in his re-education several times, there is no way but to allow him to choose his own death, so that he will be able to open a new and better page in his next incarnation.

When people realize that their lives are at risk, they will try hard to improve themselves. In this manner, there will be prevention of large public funds waste, which will then be redirected to science and progress.

In the Aquarius Age, laws will be passed to support the death penalty. Once a person is found responsible (with the help of psychics and investigators) and incriminated of taking the lives of others, he will be sentenced to death and given the opportunity to choose the manner by which he will die.

This is an age, in which all the acts of a person come back to him during his lifetime, **every person who took the life of others, his life will be taken away from him, immediately.**

Re-education

Prisons for adults and correction facilities / boarding schools for juveniles will be turned into re-education villages, as most of them are victims of society!

Most of these people grew up without an education and appropriate parental guidance. We must be compassionate toward them and not have them thrown into prolonged imprisonment sentences.

Prisons do not educate and usually have the opposite effect. Towards the Aquarius Age, hate and ignorance will be replaced with compassion and love. The frequencies of the Earth will undergo refinement, and will affect everyone. Once they are educated, they will be integrated into society with equal rights, and their past will be hidden to allow them to start new chapters in their lives.

Art and culture of beauty

In the Age of the Pisces, from which we are departing, education expanded and has intensified since the introduction of the Aquarius Age in 1638, the period of discoveries and inventions.

As we are departing from the Age of Pisces, which is the age of individual consumption, and toward the Aquarius Age, we will witness modesty, humbleness, and collective consumption.

The Aquarius Age will promote the personal art and beauty as a unique individual culture without idol-like admiration and copying, an age of love and recognition of human dignity, respect, love for the other and self-love, being accepted by yourself and the community, without the need to resemble others.

Future medicine
Science and technology in medicine

👍 **The Aquarius Age will fix the destruction of the Age of the Pisces:**

Healing and diagnosis

Since the symbol of the Aquarius sign is waves, so too are inventions of devices related to waves, such as infrared waves, ultrasound, MRI, ultraviolet, laser, and more.

The DNA medicine and the frequency medicine

Towards the spiritual Aquarius Age, a divine insight is obtained, that all diseases are originally from the soul. Therefore, it is necessary to also heal people with the help of healers and mediums who understand the true source of the problem, which is usually related to lessons from previous incarnations that a person did not complete. In every incarnation, he has the opportunity to complete lessons.

If all lessons were already completed, then he wouldn't have been born. Every person who was born came to Earth in order to complete lesson(s).

When you see people, they are actually walking lessons.

The Creation will give humanity the knowledge that everything in the universe is made-up of frequencies and every living form has its own code of frequency. In life, everything lives forever, without the ability to destroy anything. For example:

• Once you take a piece of wood, glass, metal, plastic, fabric and place it under a microscope, then you will find out that the atoms are moving! That's because everything around you is actually alive, forever. You may only exchange between states of matter.

• Every grass which will be cut or a forest that burns, will grow again naturally.

• Every lake, river, sea, ocean which will be polluted, will be cleaned again naturally.

• Every person who dies - his spirit will choose whether to reincarnate as a soul or matter (according to the enlightenment of the spirit).

• **Nothing can be killed in the universe, everything is infinite and lives forever,** it is only possible to change its state of matter.

In the Aquarius Age, thanks to advance technologies, people will have the capability to live 200 - 400 years.

With the help of biological medicine, frequency devices, advanced technology, will lead to the DNA cells and immune system to be upgraded to a high level of resistance against harmful viruses and bacteria. This will improve physical abilities and memory, metabolism and weight control, deceleration of aging, prevention and recovery from disease.

There will be control over aging, appearance of skin and hair, body aches, correction of brain waves, neutralization of physical pain, and more.

In the Aquarius Age, there won't be over the counter medicine, but only ones which are customized and matched to each person, based on his personal DNA.

Knowledge Bank: databases, memory, and knowledge

Positive property: people will be able to copy information, memory, and knowledge from one person to another using **Knowledge Banks**, especially at the end of their life, they will donate their data to the bank, in favor of the next generation. This will be done by using advanced alien technology, via electrodes which will be connected to the brain.

Before the death of a person, a 'memory will' will be made. Skills and data such as general knowledge, hobbies and leisure, music playing, cooking, languages, experiences, travels and others will be digitally deposited into the Knowledge Bank, similar to a public library, in which people can donate, borrow, or buy books.

Towards the Aquarius Age, people will be taught how to use their 10 senses, in order to heal themselves and others. (Divine Creation / 2016).

Negative property: this ability can be used as a means of power and control by corrupted people and organizations, in which they will be able to cause damage, prevent freedom, and disrupt justice by the transfer of knowledge without the consent of the person. This may lead to the corruption or deletion of memory, knowledge, or information, which will lead to the distortion of the truth.

Vaccinations and fraud of pharmaceutical companies

All vaccines are toxic and harm the immune system, which causes diseases, in order to ensure that repeat customers, constant income from repeat customers, and the dilution of population, in which the pharmaceutical industry always works with the government or vice versa.

Since the time when vaccines were administered, many diseases started to appear, such as autism, allergies, asthma, diabetes, cancer, osteoporosis, Alzheimer's, and many other diseases which didn't exist prior to administration of vaccines.

Life expectancy has NOT increased because of vaccines, but thanks to the high level of HYGIENE, which has increased considerably in the last hundred years.

In the coming Aquarius Age, vaccines will be banned and it must be through chaos, in order to create something new.

Vaccines will be banned and replaced with natural energies, like frequency and advanced alien technology.

The DNA coils will be upgraded back to the 12 basic coils, as we were created at the beginning of time.

The purposes of the vaccines are evil: to make humans become consumers of the big pharma, under the control of the corrupted governments, which need the population to be sick in order to control them and reduce their quantities.

Every person who cooperates with this evil mission, in order to take the lives of others, his life will be taken by *The Creation*, in this lifetime.

Once you receive a vaccine, you are under the control of the government, and once you refuse to receive any vaccine, then the government raises its monster head, closes you around from all sides, and stops respecting human rights using force upon the citizens leveraging the police, army, and other security forces.

We are separating gradually from the Age of the Pisces, the age of money, in which the amazing marketing phenomenon of pharmaceutical companies takes place, such as medical propagandist, mainly pretty women. Their profession is to update doctors with new medicines and convince the doctors to recommend and prescribe their company's drugs to their patients, in exchange for benefits and funding for conference trips, and more.

Once doctors are being paid-off by the pharmaceutical companies, and prescribe patients with these drugs, they help people to stay sick and remain addicted to drugs, and their lives become dependent on this supply and consumer demand system.

Please remember, every person who cooperates with this evil mission, in order to take the lives of others, his life will be taken by *The Creation*, in this lifetime.

The consumers sponsor doctors and the pharma industry. This phenomenon exists in the corrupted pharmaceutical industry worldwide. **In this way, doctors get tremendous control in one hand, and on the other one they do not take any responsibility if the medications they have prescribed did cause their patients harm or death.**

Some medicines and painkillers cause patients to become addicted to them, with potentially fatal consequences. The pharmaceutical companies, health organizations, ministry of health and governments, all cooperate together to create an industry which is sponsored by the patients, in order to control the lives and health of the population and reduce the quantity of people.

Towards the Aquarius Age, the power will return to the citizens who will expose the truth and bring justice and new way of natural health, using frequency devices and fixing the DNA. Before the pharmaceutical companies will vanish for good, they will pay for the health damage of their consumers.

Printing and manufacturing accessories and body parts will initially be prepared in personal printers and then in laboratories to produce in large quantities in a customized way for each person or animal, according to his DNA coils. This will be a rapid alternative to organ donation, which now takes long periods of waiting and is not suited to every person.

Psychics and healers, with the assistance of advanced alien technology, and other professionals will diagnose the source of the problem from the previous life of the person to determine what is the root cause, lesson, and karma of the person. They will also provide guidance for self-healing. The state of the soul, reflects the state of the physical body.

The connection between the thyroid gland and a variety of diseases

There is also a negative aspect to the spiritual Aquarius Age (Spirit), such as dramatic increase of mood swings and depressions, caused by loneliness, interacting with machines and devices, instead of humans, heredity, foods and medicine full of hormones.

Many women consume hormones, via pills, infertility treatments, and intrauterine devices, all of which disrupt the natural hormonal balance in the body and damage the glands of the endocrine systems. These are a collection of glands that produce and secrete hormones to the bloodstream which help the brain and heart, but unfortunately, this is why consuming artificial hormones causes many diseases nowadays.

The use of hormones will develop in time to hypothyroidism which attacks mainly women with many signs, such as:

• Weight gain and slowing metabolism.

• Cancer in hormonal areas, such as breast, uterus, cervix, and lymph nodes.

• Fatigue, weakness, fertility problems, and bloated stomach.

• Moods, depression, and loss of libido.

• Fractured nails, hair loss, constipation and anemia, slowed heart rate.

• Dry skin, skin dandruff, and facial swelling.

• Contractions and muscle pain, fibromyalgia, and painful joints.

• Sensitivity to cold and low calcium, sleep problems, and memory issues.

People must understand the connection between hormonal medicines and the disruption they cause to endocrine glands, especially the thyroid gland.

Women around the world suffer from these symptoms, but are mistakenly diagnosed with various diseases and provided with unnecessary prescriptions medications, without assigning these symptoms to hormonal status, resulting from long-term hormonal medicines. Sometimes, even years after stopping hormonal treatment, the body takes at least four years to clear up the body from each medicine.

The body has the ability to heal itself.

If we look back in time, the majority of people were thin, because of their healthy, organic, and nutritious diet, which was pesticide free. Physical activity was mainly walking, riding, and climbing stairs, yet no-one ran, there weren't any exercise gyms, nor workout outfits.

During the 1960's the birth control pills were marketed and since then, the thyroid gland was damaged, and the population started to become ill from obesity.

Since this period, the food industry started to produce unhealthy, inorganic, and non-nutritious foods and drinks, which led to a variety of diseases, such as diabetes, cancer, osteoporosis, Alzheimer's, and many more.

Decreased sperm quality

The quality of male sperm has been impaired with the side effects of progress, for instance, vaccinations, medicines, industrialized food, pesticides, food and milk loaded with hormones, drinking water with chemicals, sedentary work, riding, cellular radiation, stress, drugs, medicines, smoking, and more.

Humans have found a manipulative way of bypassing the natural pregnancy by IVF treatments and thus producing multiple births of twins, triplets, and more. Remember that that the quantity of souls is limited in the universe.

Each attempt to manipulate the nature, will come back to humanity, in the form of de-population.

A bank for sperm replication

In the Aquarius Age, the power of women will grow worldwide, they will lead revolutions, and establish many communities, along with world peace. Women will reach the conclusion that they don't need men to bring offspring.
An advanced sperm bank will be established, which will replicate and improve the DNA of the male sperm and the egg of the female.

Due to the technological ability to upgrade the DNA, it will be possible for the customer to choose the external appearance, physical and mental strength of the newborn, with the **option** of leveraging artificial futuristic incubators, which will replace the woman's pregnancy process.

Towards the Aquarius Age, babies with high abilities, advanced capabilities, without physical and mental diseases, will be born.

As we enter the Aquarius Age, people will live in communities, many of them will be exclusive to women. The status of men will decline, and there will be struggles between the genders throughout the age.

Death and Burial

In the Age of the Pisces, death was treated as a terrible thing, conversations about death were silenced, humanitarian death and the right to die with dignity were not honored, and preparations for death were not given to the deceased and their loved ones.

Death and birth are fixed stations for every soul that resides in a temporary physical body of matter.

Why do people celebrate the birth of a baby and mourn at the time of death?

Every living creature has an expiration date! Humanity must celebrate both holidays: birth and death!

At Birth:

the soul enters a physical body chosen by itself.

When? During the baby's first breath during delivery.
The spirit chooses a temporary body (material) and then the soul resides in it.
No physical body may contain two souls together at the same time; therefore, a pregnant woman cannot inhabit two souls in her body, otherwise it would be considered as if she is possessed.

Therefore, abortion is not considered murder.

At the time of death:

the soul leaves the physical body that it has chosen and returns to its original state, as an infinite spirit with knowledge and experience. **The soul can descend / ascend into the world of matter and spirit,** as was described in my first book, Divine Creation.

In the approaching Aquarius Age, many will deal with death:

• Each person will be able to choose when and how to end his life. The community will make all the arrangements for the deceased, including cremation. Each community will bear these costs.

• Psychics and healers will be integrated into the public health systems and will mainly work with advanced alien technology.

• As there is a preparation for birth counselor, with the help of midwives, so a new profession will be created, a counselor who will be in charge of the preparation for death, with the help of psychics and healers.

• Conversations with the spirits of deceased, entities, aliens, and other life forms from other planets, will be made by psychics and will become common. Gradually, this ability will become natural for everyone.

In the arrival of the Aquarius Age, an insight will be given to humanity:

"You cannot die, you do not die but exchange host body, each one has an endless spirit"

Tombstones, ceremonies, and memorial days will be banned as they will be considered ancient pagan phenomenon. There is no need to worship matter, because the spirit is endless and can never die. The expensive lands of the cemeteries will be used by the living, and not for the purpose of burying new corpses, which will be cremated.

In order give the expensive lands of cemeteries to the living, old corpses will be removed from the ground, cremated, and the ashes and the stones will be given to their families, and all the expenses will be paid by the community.

There will be an option for any person to choose pre-death what shall be done with his ashes, to keep it in urns, to spread it back to the nature, or to plant a tree on top of the ashes, which will be mixed with dirt, or other options based on the person's choice.

Every creation requires chaos; thus, a huge worldwide chaos is expected, in order to create these benefits for future generations.

As the bible mentions, "To ashes you shall return", refers to cremation because a corpse in the ground does not become ashes, but remains a skeleton.

The Aquarius Age will start to create a logical world.

Comparison tables between ages #1

Subject	From the Age of the Pisces	to the Age of the Aquarius
Zodiac sign	Water, control, power, and ego.	Air, freedom, compassion, and justice.
Science and technologies	With water. Sailing, steam.	Air, gas and aviation combined with spirituality.
Spirituality	Faith in material: religions, tombstones, and coercion.	Free faith.
Leadership	Men rule by power and wars.	Communities with female leadership, who will maintain world peace.
	Dictators, queens, and governments, using forced control.	Communities will protect the citizens, without forced control.
	Singles, dynasties, and monarchs.	Masses, communities.
Governments	Multiple.	World-wide communities

Human Rights	Slavery and inequality between the genders, religion, and nationality.	Equal rights to all citizens.
Penalties	Boarding schools, institutions, Prisons, and prolonged imprisonment.	Rural re-education, and choosing the way to die.

Comparison tables between ages # 2

Subject	From the Age of the Pisces	to the Age of the Aquarius
Education and knowledge	Strict and defined by classes, grades, and degrees.	Freedom, cooperative society, without grades and titles.
Consumption culture	Abundance, brands, and waste.	Modesty and recycling.
Language	Multi-language.	International language: English.
Medicine	By doctors and pharmaceutical medicines.	Psychics, healers, advanced alien technology, frequencies, and medical DNA.
Contests and sports	Prizes and glorification of the ego.	Without competition and prizes, Community unification.
Between countries	Borders and entry visas.	Without borders and visas. Freedom of movement.
Environment	Pollution and destruction of natural reservoirs.	Repairing, healing, and preserving all nature and

THE AQUARIUS AGE   173

		animals.
Finance	Money, material, wealth for individuals and corruption.	Virtual currency, knowledge trading, barter, and corruption-free justice.
Consumption	Increased imports and brands. Massive waste.	Barter, limited, humbleness, and modest, using the existing and recycling.

Comparison tables between ages # 3

Subject	From the Age of the Pisces	to the Age of the Aquarius
Life and occupation	A family cell, single or a couple with / without children. Employees or self-employment.	Community living cells. Everyone is self-employed, dealing with the community.
Euthanasia	Is prohibited and restricted in most countries.	The freedom to die with dignity for every applicant and at any age.
Birthrate and population	Population growth, birth unregulated.	Parental license to have children.
Birth and death	Mid-wives, preparation for birth, preventing the freedom to die.	Mid-wives and death counselors, Preparation for birth and death, choosing the way to die, conversations with deceased.
Burial	To be buried in the ground, in a coffin with tombstone.	Cremating the body, place ashes in urns, spread it in nature, or plant tree above it.

Eating	Animals, pesticides, non-nutritious foods, white flour, sugar, and substitutes.	Vegetarianism, veganism, healthy eating, fiber-rich, and natural sweetener.
Nature	Slavery, abuse, lack of respect for life and nature.	Respect, protection and compassion for all nature and all around.
Earth frequencies	Rigid frequencies: power, destruction, male ego, wars, and injustice.	Subtle frequencies: justice, unity, compassion, insight, peace, and mutual respect.

Summary

The Creators (aliens) created humanity (*The Created*) here on Earth.

The purpose of spirit:
For the actions of the soul in the material body to attest to the nature of God / *The Creation.*

The purpose of the material:
For humans to become creators themselves and to create other advanced emotional human beings.

Your mission is to create upgraded, emotional, compassionate humanity, in order to continue the infinite engine of *The Creation.*

***The Creation* will always allow
freedom of choice
from at least two,
in order to provide free choice.
Therefore, God will never be one.**

Dear readers,

For further reading, you are welcome to read my other two books, which were also channeled through me by *The Creation Entities* and I typed them directly into the computer:

1. **Divine Creation:**
   offers the readers with the meaning of life, who is God / *The Creation, The Creators, The Created*. Who created humanity on Earth? What is the purpose of humanity? and many other topics and insights.

2. **The Future:**
   provides the readers with astrological and numerological research and information regarding how the Zodiac aligns with the pages of history. In this research, I moved in time 4,000 years backwards and 25,000 years forward, and discovered there is a mathematical pattern, which has allowed humanity to understand what happened in the past and predict the future, according to the Zodiac movement.

The circle of life has no beginning or end, nothing can be destroyed, yet you can only change the states of matter.

You are a spirit embodied in a temporary material body as a soul, while your actions testify to the nature of God.

As I wrote at the beginning of this book, don't believe the contents of this book, yet create your own truth, because there will never be a single truth, in order to provide you with a free choice.

Take this book's insights as a different approach, from here you can explore and enrich your own life.

You are welcome to listen to my frequency singing, while *The Creation Entities* also channeled through me, as it reaches the soul, relaxes, and heals, on my **YouTube Channel** and website www.Gali4u.com.

Copyright © 2021 Gali Lucy Nadiv

About the author

Gali Lucy

Medium, Author, and Architecture Engineer, who channels with *The Creation's Entities* since the age of six. She channels through her brain without any additional tools and advises on a variety of topics world-wide.

She gained vast experience and positive reputation for accuracy in predicting the future, both on a personal and global level, using X-ray remote vision ability.

She is the author of the following spiritual books:
1. Divine Creation
2. The Future
3. The Aquarius Age

These books were dictated to her through channeling with an easy and simple explanation and information, regarding what is *The Creation's* plan for humanity on planet Earth and to prepare mankind into the entrance of the Aquarius Age.

She also sings frequency songs without background music in her **Gali Lucy** <u>**YouTube Channel**</u>, while *The Creation's Entities* are channeling through her.

Author Website: <u>www.Gali4u.com.</u>

Made in the USA
Middletown, DE
01 June 2021

40794426R00102